ANYWHERE BUT HERE

Travellers in Camden

Mary Daly

Published by the London Race and Housing Research Unit
c/o the Runnymede Trust, 11 Princelet Street, London E1 6QH
April 1990
© London Race and Housing Research Unit
Designed by David Rosenberg
Typeset and printed by the Russell Press, Nottingham

Contents

Photographs:
Page 6, 21 *Jenny O'Brien (Format)*
Page 43, 69, 72 *Chris Taylor*

Acknowledgements

I would like to acknowledge the contribution made to this report by the following:

Errol Lawrence and Sabes Sugunasabesan of the London Race & Housing Research Unit who provided the funding for the project and support and advice throughout.

The Steering Group to the Project: from its commencement the Steering Group included Patricia Back, Brian Miller, Tom Kiernan, Stephen Cawley and members of the Camden Irish Workers Group. Particular thanks are due to Maggie Pether, Anne Godfrey and Kevin McCarthy, who supported the project throughout.

All the Travellers who took part in this research and shared their experiences.

Terri Suddaby and Michael McCann, interviewer and consultant to the research.

Staff of Camden Homeless Persons Section.
Camden Council Central Race Relations Unit, especially Jennifer Weekes.
Camden HASSL.
Camden Womens Aid.
Homeless Families Play Team.
The Irish Centre.
London Housing Forum — June Spencer.
Linda Dodge, Health Visitor for Travellers.
Susan Rumney — Director of Community Nursing, Bloomsbury Health Authority.
Seamus Taylor — Haringey Irish Project.
Bayswater Hotel Homeless Project.
Father Daly — Chaplain to Travellers in Britain.

Mary Daly

Preface

This report gives an account of the findings of a research project looking into discrimination against homeless Travellers in the London Borough of Camden.

The report was commissioned by Camden Council's Race Unit in October 1986, because they had indications that homeless Travellers were experiencing discrimination. The project was set up to research the extent of such discrimination and to make recommendations to the Council's Race Committee. Funding and management were provided, respectively, by the London Race and Housing Research Unit and Camden Council.

The Report reflects the fact that the severity of the discrimination faced by Irish Travellers in Camden increased dramatically and took new forms during the period of the research, as a result of deliberate policy decisions made by Camden Council.

The research was carried out between July 1987 and March 1988 — a period of unprecedented confusion and change in Camden Council that profoundly affected the circumstances in which the researcher was working. The lives of the people she was researching were being devastated by the ensuing chaos.

Mary Daly the researcher found that the Travellers she met were deeply sceptical about research into their "plight". From their viewpoint it was all too clear what should happen. Camden should stop discriminating against them, start implementing its own policies and provide a roof over their heads. In these circumstances the task of retaining the confidence of Travellers whilst maintaining a detached and independent view of their conditions — both prerequisites to effective research — required Mary Daly to tread delicately along a thin line.

This delicate balance is reflected in the writing of the report. The continual tension between the role of independent researcher and that of advocate for Travellers human rights expresses itself in the different "voices" in which the report is written. Another aspect of the way the report is presented is that the section describing policy changes follows that on the Research findings. This order was chosen because there was no defined context within which the Travellers could locate their experiences in Camden. Therefore it was decided that their experiences should be related before the policies of the Council were examined.

One of Mary Daly's key findings is that the Council exaggerated the number of homeless Irish Travellers and indeed that the Council had little idea as to the real scale of the "problem". Faced with a growing homelessness crises and a catastrophic budget deficit Camden Council sought to explain its inability to meet its responsibilities in what could be seen as a classic racist manner. It swiftly moved to suggest that here was a group of people who did not deserve a service, could be excluded from it and blamed for the budget deficit. Travellers, in Camden, were to be the scapegoats just as the Bangladeshi families were in Tower Hamlets. Conveniently, or perhaps miraculously, Camden Council estimated to the *Daily Mail* that it was spending £11m on homeless Irish Travellers — exactly the figure of its homeless budget overspend. The racist manipulation of statistics to obscure the real source of problems and the targeting and blaming of a particular group for those problems has a long and infamous history. Enoch Powell's notorious 1968 "rivers of blood" speech is a relatively recent example; matched more recently still by Prime Minister Thatcher's use of the term "swamping" to describe black immigration.

The Race Relations Act 1976, section 71, imposes a statutory duty on local authorities "to make appropriate arrangements with a view to securing that their various functions are carried out with due regard to the need (a) to eliminate unlawful racial discrimination and (b) to promote equality of opportunity and good relations between persons of different racial groups". Camden, along with some other London Councils, has gained kudos in some quarters, and notoriety in others for its ethnic minority policies. In view of this, the way in which Camden treated Irish Travellers may come as a surprise to some. In fact the research found that Camden's much-trumpeted anti-racist policies were unable to withstand the impact of Government financial constraints. When these began to bite, the Council's veneer of liberalism cracked, exposing a set of all too familiar imperialist attitudes and responses. At best Camden displayed a lack of political will to pursue its own policies when the going got tough. Whatever the Council's intentions the effects of its actions were consistent with the review that Irish and other ethnic minority groups deserve worse treatment than other members of the community. The material reality of Traveller's lives make it difficult for them to organise and resist. Camden by it's actions appeared to be taking advantage of that fact.

This report gives those people a voice.

Camden Travellers and Homeless Research Project Steering Group

1. Background

This report is the result of a eight month research period and, as such, it does not seek to provide in-depth analysis or quantitative findings, but rather, to raise questions, and make links between the various issues that have contributed to the situation of homeless Travellers in the London Borough of Camden. The report does not provide a definitive picture of the situation of homeless Travellers everywhere, but is rooted in time and place in Camden over that eight month period.

During 1986 Camden Council's Central Race Relations Unit became concerned that Traveller families were experiencing discrimination both in their contact with Homeless Persons Service (HPS), and in their experiences of living in Bed and Breakfast (B&B) hotels and Stage II Accommodation.

On 15 January 1986, the Police were called to Camden Homeless Persons Service to remove a Travelling family, who had refused to leave the building. The family had been offered a hotel in the Tavistock Square DHSS Area, and had refused to take it because of difficulties experienced by Travellers with the DHSS in this area. Having been removed from the building the family stayed outside. The Police were called a second time and the parents of the three children were arrested for refusing to leave. A Place of Safety Order was taken out on the three children who were placed with foster parents. The mother was charged with assault on the baby and neglect, the father was charged with neglect of the three children. The following day the parents appeared in court and were remanded until 23 January.

Meanwhile the children were taken to a General Practitioner who observed that they were recovering from chicken pox. A paediatrician's opinion was sought on this and on the Police allegation of neglect. The children were thoroughly examined, by a paediatrician at University College Hospital, Euston, London, who reported that he had no concerns about their growth, and considered the children to be well nourished. He

1

could find "no serious abnormalities and certainly no evidence of Non-Accidental Injury".

After this examination, the Police applied for and were granted, an Interim Care Order, as the Place of Safety Order had expired, and the parents were not appearing in the Magistrates Court for another two days.

At a Social Services Department case conference held on 22 January, it was decided that there was no evidence for the children to be placed on the Child Protection Register and that they would be returned to their parents. If the parents were refused bail, they should be discharged into the care of grandparents. The Police were not to seek a Care Order, and Social Services would explain in Court the position of the children and recommend that they be discharged into the care of their parents.

This family's experience at the hands of Camden Homeless Persons Service, made a travesty out of the Council's policy on Travellers which stated that:

"... all Council Departments are asked to endorse a non-harassment policy towards Travellers and to ensure that they are not acting in a discriminatory way towards Travellers". (3.b) *see Appendix I*

This incident, along with many complaints from Travellers in HPS temporary accommodation that they were being discriminated against, as well as the lack of concrete information about Traveller's experience of homelessness and their housing needs, prompted the Central Race Relations Unit to seek funding for this research project.

In the first week of the research I met with several HPS staff, who acknowledged the inadequacy of B&B Accommodation for Traveller families. The HPS had had one training session about Travellers.

The main problems appeared to be:
— Not staying in hotels, moving away or returning again months later to present as homeless.
— Hotels will not take Traveller families on grounds that they are a 'nuisance'.
— Travellers tend to turn up in groups of families which is too much to accommodate at one time, and the system cannot handle this.
— Children are a nuisance in hotels and in HPS reception areas.
— Problems with lack of literacy.
— Travellers generally want to be on the ground floor and this is not often possible.
— Lack of trust between Travellers and Advisers — suspicion on both sides.

2

— Allocating housing to Travellers is difficult because often they disagree among themselves and one family may not want to live close to another family. In this case HPS take the view that it is the choice of the families concerned if they decide to move out of the area for these types of reasons.

Thus Travellers had come to be perceived as a 'problem' instead of the focus being on the ways in which HPS policy and practice falls short of meeting Travellers' needs. This posed the question as to whether a service exists to meet the needs of its clients, or whether certain groups with particular needs come to be seen as a problem because their needs do not conform to those of the majority of the people using the service. I spoke to the HPS manager about why Travellers are perceived in this way and was informed that when Travellers first began presenting as homeless, they were considered 'delightful' by HPS staff. Travellers began to be seen as a problem when the numbers presenting as homeless increased. Staff began to 'feel' that the system was being abused. 'Rumours were going around' that Travellers were only using hotels as an easier route to money from the DHSS and staff resented the way Travellers sometimes did not stay in hotels after they had been booked in. In the view of the staff this caused other homeless people to suffer, while the Travellers concerned could find somewhere else to stay. Staff became frustrated because they could not understand what Travellers wanted. It was also difficult to place Travellers in hotels because some hotels would not have them. Because Travellers were not used to hotel life this caused problems. There had also been incidents of racial abuse to individual HPS staff from particular Travellers and incidents of violence in the reception area which had led to a "siege mentality" among staff.

Given that the 'problems' were so clearly defined by HPS and had been for some time, I enquired as to what positive initiatives HPS had taken regarding improving their service to Travellers and easing the pressure on the HPS staff.

There had been plans to employ a Travellers Outreach Worker in the HPS but by this time there was 'no chance' of this happening because of the squeeze on Council resources. This Research project, which was commissioned by the Central Race Relations Unit was also cited as a positive response!

Mary Daly
Researcher, Travellers & Homelessness Project, Central Race Relations Unit, London Borough of Camden

3

2. Travellers in Camden — the wider context

Before looking at the position of homeless Travellers it is necessary to place the Camden situation in a wider context, and look at a number of issues which have affected the life of Camden's Travelling Community: contemporary emigration from Ireland and conditions Travellers face in Ireland; the changes in the Travelling lifestyle in Britain over the last few decades; the impact of the Caravan Sites Act (1968) and more recently the Public Order Act (1986) and Camden's non-harassment policy towards the Travelling Community.

Ireland

Emigration — a lesson in survival
Travellers have been coming to Camden for many years. In the course of the research project all the Travellers contacted were Irish. This is not surprising given that the Irish Community in Camden is both large and well-established, and that contemporary emigration from Ireland has added substantially to that community. Although emigration levels are not monitored, the Irish Embassy in London estimate that between 1982-87 at least 75,000 people emigrated from Ireland into Britain. Some sources would suggest that the figures are more alarming, and that in 1986 alone, up to 50,000 people entered Britain. Amongst these immigrants, are a significant number of Travelling people who are no longer able to sustain a living in Ireland, where, despite emigration, more than 19 per cent of the total workforce are unemployed.

Emigration is nothing new to the Irish. Between 1946-1971 1,300,000 people emigrated from Ireland and 80 per cent of these settled in Britain. The majority of these immigrants faced a hostile reception and had to struggle for survival within an alien community. Although their resources were utilised in the rebuilding of Britain after the war, they found themselves in poor housing in the big cities, and in low paid manual work. Although life at that time was far from easy, there was more possibility of employment albeit poorly paid and back breaking, than there is for the contemporary Irish immigrant. The Irish entering Britain today find a society which is shedding all concern for its most disadvantaged and vulnerable members. Many of them are unable to find work, or if they do, cannot find accommodation. In London the accommodation situation is particularly acute, and many Irish immigrants find themselves homeless. They also have to contend with the effects of Britain's colonial enterprises in Ireland in the form of harassment under the Prevention of Terrorism Act and Anti-Irish racism, leading to widespread discrimination. This is bad enough, but for Irish Travellers the burdens are enormous. They also have to contend with hostility from within the Irish community, as well as the host community. They have very few legal stopping places and are continuously scapegoated and attacked and must find a way of surviving, while their lifestyle and identity as Travelling people is being squeezed from all sides.

Travelling in Ireland
Most of the Travellers who contributed to this research have come to Britain because they cannot afford to live and look after their families in Ireland. What follows are actual experiences of Travellers related personally to the researcher in Ireland. The position for Travellers in Ireland is far from satisfactory. Where there are sites, they tend to be located in isolated places, far away from shops, schools, and local amenities and conditions tend to be primitive. Chalets are provided on site, and when one family moves out, another family is expected to move in immediately often with no repair work or redecoration being done on the chalet. This does not happen usually to settled people living in council houses. Often the chalets are badly built with poor insulation and no damp-proofing. A typical site in Dublin was built miles from any facilities, on a sinking foundation. Families could not live in the chalets because of mould growing on the walls, and there was only one stove for heating for the whole chalet. On another site, the chalets were pre-fabricated, with asbestos in the walls. In these, the only sink available was in the toilet, and there was one bedroom provided for the whole family. This indicates the type of provision made in Ireland for Travellers. In the late 1970s an independent body of Travellers called *Minceir Misli* formed a Committee to campaign for Travellers Rights.[1] This body made demands to local and central government for halting sites. Protests were held outside *Dail*

Traveller in Belfast

Eireann (the Irish Parliament) but to no avail. It is the view of most of the Travellers I spoke to that they are without legal rights in Ireland.

When any accommodation is made available to Travellers, reaction from local residents tends to be violently hostile, with Travellers often being physically attacked with sticks and crowbars or petrol-bombs being thrown onto the site and through the windows of trailers. If the Travellers attempt to defend themselves and the police arrive on the scene, it is often the Travellers who are arrested and charged when their only crime has been trying to defend their families from attack. When Travellers move into Council housing they are not accepted by their neighbours who demonstrate with placards saying they do not want Travellers in the area. This type of anti-Traveller activity is not haphazard, but tends to be well organised. Where Travellers live in houses, they experience overt discrimination from the local community, often being refused service in local shops and denied access to facilities and places of entertainment.

Because of the severe economic recession in Ireland, there is less work for Travellers, and they are forced to rely more on state benefit, which means 'signing on' every week. Some of the people interviewed for this research described how if a Traveller is on a site in one area and is evicted before getting time to notify the Labour Exchange, they lose their money and have to go through a lengthy appeals procedure and make a fresh claim.

In between times, the family has no money to live on, and no sympathy or consideration is given to how they are supposed to manage, often with large families and small children. Some Travellers described how, when they ask for money for things like blankets, clothes and furniture, they are repeatedly put off, until eventually it is forgotten about, or they stop trying.

When Travellers pull their trailers on to Corporation land,[2] they are told to move on, and next morning at 6am they are towed out, with the Police on hand to make sure nobody raises a protest. If you protest, say the Travellers, you get arrested. If you protest verbally you are charged with using abusive language, regardless of whether or not you did. It has been the experience of many Travellers that on arrival at the police station, they are physically assaulted and there is no word about it, because it is their word against that of the Police.

When they arrived in London, Travellers find that things are often not much better. Some Travellers we spoke to said that as bad as it was for Travellers in Ireland, it was worse in London.

England and Wales
Legislation
In England and Wales there is legislation which apparently grants Travellers some of the rights they are denied in Ireland. The Caravan Sites Act 1968 recognises the right to "a nomadic way of life" and places a duty on local authorities to make provision for Travellers in their area. However, since the Enclosure Acts[3] through to the 1959 Highways Act the thrust of legislation concerning Travellers has been to force settlement and conformity; to make a nomadic way of life so untenable that Travellers will abandon their ways and settle into houses. It is ironic that (as this research will show) Travellers who do decide to settle down and become housedwellers experience just as much discrimination and difficulty as they do pursuing their traditional lifestyle.

The Caravan Sites Act (1968)
This Act started life as a liberal measure with the intention of providing a variety of sites — permanent, temporary and halting sites throughout England and Wales, which would provide accommodation for all Travellers, whatever their particular needs. To get the legislation through

7

Parliament and gain the co-operation of reluctant local authorities concessions were made, the major one being the inclusion of the concept of "designation".

Designation

Though the act firmly places a duty on local authorities to provide adequate accommodation for Travellers "resorting to or residing in their area", the Secretary of State is given the power to grant designation on the grounds that either a local authority has made adequate provision (in London, the Act defines "adequate" as a 15 pitch site); or that there is no need to make provision or that it is "not expedient" for the local authority to provide (for example because of lack of land).

Designation is a powerful tool for local authorities because it gives them the power to apply to the Magistrates Court for an order to remove Travellers, occupying land without permission, within 24 hours. If they fail to move when ordered the Travellers are committing a criminal offence.

Effectively, this is akin to the operation of a pass law, because it imposes a restriction upon the number of Travellers who reside legally within the boundaries of the local state. Of the 32 London Boroughs, 20 have been granted designation under the Act, which means that Travellers freedom of movement is severely curtailed across London. It has been rightly argued that the Caravan Sites Act (1968), criminalises Travelling peoples' very way of life.

The Act is shortsighted also insofar as that even if a London borough has provided an official 15 pitch site, as required by the law, this does not solve the problem of accommodation which arises for the children of those people living on the site. Where are they supposed to go when they grow up and want to have families of their own? If they want to maintain the Travelling way of life then they are forced into camping illegally on land in the locality because insufficient provision has been made for them. In their eagerness to obtain designation powers local authorities have provided the bare minimum of permanent pitches, or in many cases nothing at all, and an increasing population of Travellers is faced with a decreasing supply of legal sites, and further legislation aimed primarily at curbing their lifestyle.

The Public Order Act (1986)

Since the introduction of the Public Order Act (1986) the situation Travellers find themselves in has worsened. Section 39 of the Act imposed a limited offence of Criminal Trespass. The offence of Criminal Trespass is open to being used in a discriminatory way against Travellers in that it applies specifically to "two or more persons" (ie groups of people) who have moved around.

Section 39 gives to the Police the power to direct Travellers to move off a piece of land on being requested to do so by the landowners. Prior to the legislation landowners used the civil procedure which gives Travellers notice and the right to a defence in Court without the liability of arrest for a criminal offence.

There is no acknowledgement within the Public Order Act of a right to a nomadic way of life, which would appear to contradict the establishment of this right by the Caravan Sites Act (1968).

One of the first examples of the use of the Public Order Act in Camden occurred when British Rail used it to remove Travellers from their land in the Borough.

On this occasion when British Rail were asked why they were not using civil procedure as they had always done in the past, the reply was that British Rail now realised that they could be "quicker off the mark" by using Section 39.

The Police did not explain the provisions of the Public Order Act to the Travellers concerned, but simply told them to leave. The Travellers were expecting to be dealt with as on a previous occasion by being given Notice to Quit under the civil procedure. Instead they were given 10 minutes to leave otherwise they would be charged with a new offence of criminal trespass under Section 39 of the Public Order Act and the Police refused to give any more time than this.

The Travellers refused to go and several of them and their children were arrested and their vehicles towed onto the highway. They were held overnight in custody because they had no fixed address and their children were placed in the care of Camden Social Services.

In Court the solicitor acting for them advised the Travellers that if they pleaded not guilty and asked for time to organise their defence on the basis that the Police were acting unlawfully, under the Public Order Act they would certainly be remanded in custody, having no fixed address. It is hardly surprising that the Travellers decided to plead guilty. In these circumstances it was their only option if they wanted to prevent their children remaining in care.

The solicitor tried to show that the Travellers were unaware of the provisions of Section 39 and that in the circumstances they had no option but to trespass. He also put before the Magistrates, the situation for

Travellers in London, and especially in Camden itself, where there are no official sites.

The Magistrates imposed a fine of £25 each or seven days in prison. The Travellers paid their fines and were released.

In Camden the failure of the Public Order Act to acknowledge the right to a nomadic way of life, also contradicts the Council's own policy which recognises this right and pledges itself to make it effective through the provision of sites for the Travelling Community.

As long as Camden's policy exists, Section 39 cannot be used by the police to arrest and evict Travellers from Council land, because in the case of an eviction being sought it is Camden's policy to use civil procedures.

If Camden fail to maintain the non-harassment policy and decide to evict Travellers speedily off Council land, then it is a very real possibility that Section 39 of the Public Order Act would be used.

A changing experience

The cry often goes up from house-dwellers who find a Travellers Site near them, that if they were "proper gypsies" it would be all right. The notion of "proper gypsies" draws on a vision of the Travelling life which no longer exists, and which has become a romantic stereotype. The mention of 'gypsies' in this context evokes a picture of colourful people sat around a camp fire, telling stories and making handicrafts. This does not correspond at all with the reality of the life of an urban Traveller in the late 1980s. Travellers have moved into the cities in search of a livelihood since the 1950s. What was once a predominantly rural lifestyle, has been changed by the increased mechanisation on farms which has taken away the need of seasonal agricultural labour, once a major source of income for Travellers. Similarly the easy availability of cheap, mass produced household goods has undermined the traditional employment of Travellers. In addition, improved roads has meant less possibility of roadside encampments, which in any case became a definite thing of the past with the 1959 Highways Act. This Act made it an offence for Travellers to camp by the road or on a layby. All of this, along with the move away from horse drawn wagons to the modern cars, vans, lorries, and trailers, means that the Travellers' way of life has shifted from a rural to an urban base.

In search of work such as tarmac-adam laying, dealing in scrap metal, and selling various goods, Travellers increasingly find themselves in the heart of the inner city, in close proximity to the settled house-dwellers, who, as soon as Travellers became their neighbours quickly forget any previous idea they may have had of "live and let live".

In London, it is a common sight to see "NO TRAVELLERS" signs displayed in pubs and shops and Travellers are discriminated against with regard to welfare benefits, housing, health and schooling in ways similar to those experienced the black and ethnic minority communities. The Commission for Racial Equality have expressed the view that Travellers are an ethnic minority within the meaning of the Race Relations Act 1976. This advice is currently being tested in the Courts and it remains to be seen whether Travellers will be able to benefit from the anti-discrimination laws of this country.[4]

Regardless of whether such blatant and pervasive discrimination is acknowledged by the State, it is clear by the very fact that discrimination is so rife that local authorities are able to evade their responsibilities under the Caravan Sites Act. By this means Travellers are denied their entitlement to the very basic human right of shelter.

3. Doing the research

The research began on July 20th 1987 and was to last six months in all. The first three months of the project were to be spent interviewing Travellers in Bed and Breakfast and Stage II Accommodation. These interviews would look at the characteristics of the homeless household and the circumstances which led to homelessness, and record the Travellers' experience of being homeless as well as their experience of the service from Camden Homeless Persons Section (HPS) and their ultimate goal. By presenting the point of view of the Travellers, the research aimed to offer a different perspective to that already available to the Council. This was felt to be important because Travellers are usually constructed as 'the problem', because they do not fit smoothly into a system which is hostile to their lifestyle and takes a poor view of their particular needs. In addition, attention needed to be given to the institution providing a service, which may be failing to meet the needs of Travelling families presenting as homeless.

With this in mind, the following six weeks of the project were to be spent observing procedures in Camden HPS, interviewing members of staff, and reviewing the written policy of the Section, with an eye to identifying any actual or potential discriminatory policies and practices. The last six weeks was to be spent writing up the project and making recommendations.

The research also aimed to find out what the view of/attitude towards, Travellers of B&B managers and Stage II managers was, and what this meant in terms of how they treat Travellers who live on their estates and in their hotels. It was decided to try and incorporate this in the first part of the project.

Difficulties encountered
This was an ambitious plan in terms of what can actually be achieved in

six months. As the project progressed it soon became evident that it was not going to run as neatly as the initial plan had suggested, and a number of issues had arisen in the first six weeks which radically changed the manner in which the research continued.

One of these was the effect on the project of not having a functioning Steering Group. Before the research began a number of people, including Travellers living in Camden, had been invited to be on the project's Steering Group. There were considerable difficulties however in getting the Steering Group off the ground and this had serious implications regarding the lack of accountability of the project to the Travelling Community. This was pointed out by the Travellers, and while attempts were being made to resolve this situation, it was requested that interviews in hotels be suspended. It was decided after a number of meetings, that a new Steering Group be established and that a Traveller be employed as a consultant to the research for the duration of the project. It was crucial to the success of the research that this should happen. Travellers' experience of discrimination by Councils and their officials made them understandably suspicious that they were being offered more promises and no action; a research project rather than basic amenities.

It took from 10 September 1987 to 12 November to get a Steering Group together. During this time it was decided to try and work on the part of the research concerned with the HPS with a view to coming back to the interviewing at a later date.

One of the features of the project however was that it was constantly being overtaken by events. For instance, Camden HPS had been closed to the public since April 1987 and despite claims that it would reopen within weeks of the start of the research, it did not. This meant that observing in HPS and interviewing staff in this context proved impossible.

Part of the research time was to have been spent reviewing the written policy of the HPS in relation to Travellers and identifying any potentially discriminatory practices. In mid-September I spent time in the HPS trying to do this. It was difficult to procure HPS policy because there was no such thing as a policy file in the Section. I had to gather together everything that passed for written policy from members of staff and work from there. Within a week of beginning this work, however, major policy changes took place in Camden which were to have a huge impact on the service received by Travellers presenting as homeless in the Borough.

Between mid-September and the beginning of December the research time was spent trying to keep up with changing events and following the effects on Travellers of policy decisions and the continued closure of the

13

HPS. This was a frustrating task, because those Travellers who were turned away by telephone were invisible, unless they contacted an advice agency or the Law Centre about their situation. Some of the things that did happen to Travellers in this time included families wandering around Kings Cross with nowhere to go; in the case of one family sleeping on the floor of the bar in the Irish Centre, while other families were booked into hotels by other agencies in the Borough, who were placed under tremendous pressure by the continued closure of the HPS to the public.

Reviewing initial aims and completing the project

Once the Steering Group began to meet, the initial aims of the project had to be reviewed in the light of the time that had elapsed and how much time was left. It was decided to seek an extension to the research time to make up for the time spent on re-establishing the project. On 3 December, funding was secured for the project to run for an extra six weeks and to employ a consultant for the duration. This pushed the completion date forward to 2 March and meant the project could resume hotel interviews.

Because of the months that had gone by since the first batch of interviews had been carried out, it was necessary to begin again by locating Travellers in hotels through the HPS Card Index.[5] This left eight to nine weeks to complete the interviews. The Steering Group decided that the time left should be spent on interviewing Travellers and Stage II Estates Managers and writing up the findings. It was agreed to discontinue interviewing hotel managers for reasons I will go into later. However, the consultant had to go back to Ireland after only three weeks, and this placed another strain on the project. However, we did manage to employ another interviewer, who had already worked with Travellers in another context, to complete the number of interviews needed to make the research credible, and the project was completed in this way.

Interviewing
Locating the families

The largest part of the research time was spent interviewing Traveller families living in Bed and Breakfast and Stage II Accommodation about their experience of homelessness.

The first step was locating the families through the Homeless Persons Section records. The manual administrative systems of the HPS in use at the time have been described as:

". . . chaotic eg the White Card System. There is no one in HPS with the responsibility for an overview of all systems . . . This leads to duplication of work, lack of information to process cases and in some cases, situations where people are left in B&B without any re-housing follow-up work being done".
(Co-ordinator's Report, Supplementary Agenda, Homelessness Member Level Meeting, June 24th 1987.)

This White Card System had to be, however, the starting point for locating the families. Its problems are discussed later.

HPS staff had estimated that in July 1987 there were in excess of 100 Traveller families placed in emergency temporary accommodation by Camden. Their way of identifying Traveller families was by their last names and the size of the family. For the purposes of this research it was decided to identify Traveller families by going on the information given by themselves, and written on their referral cards under "last place lived". Usually this gave an address of a site either in Ireland or in Britain, or simply said "Travelling" or caravan. For a variety of reasons, Camden HPS does not have any working ethnic monitoring system, and the system it is supposed to have does not in any case have a 'category' which relates to Travellers. Under these circumstances, using the information given by the Travellers themselves seemed the nearest thing to self-identification available. The drawbacks with this method are that not all Travellers live in a caravan or on a site, and some may have been living either in B&B hotels or some other kind of temporary accommodation prior to presenting as homeless in Camden, so they would not necessarily be identifiable as Travellers by the criteria adopted in this research.

The White Card system itself was a challenge. Some Cards were clearly written and easy to read. Some were indecipherable in places and had been amended so often that they were impossible to understand, while others had gaps in the information they contained, for instance — no last address or no referral date. Having gone through the White Card Index, the next job was to cross-check with the non-residence file and the reception day-book. Both of these should contain information about cancellations and moves from one hotel to another which would complement the information in the White Card Index. This proved a useless exercise, because neither the non-residence file nor the day-book had been used to consistently record information either about moves from one hotel to another or cancellations. Instead the information was recorded in a haphazard way, for instance some staff wrote only a date and a family's surname, which made it impossible to clearly identify different families with the same surname.

The other way to identify how many homeless people were in B&B and where they were located was to turn to the current hotels occupation list.

Potentially this list contains information under the following headings:

Name and Initials; Room Number; Case Number; Adults; Preg; 0-4; 5-10; 11+; Date of Homelessness; Date placed; Team; Date Out; Order Numbers; Comments.

The list is useful for estimating total B&B occupation, but to try and identify Traveller families is impossible, unless a cross-check is made with names, size of family and case numbers. This would have been feasible if the hotels list had consistently contained the information it was supposed to. In reality, the family's initials and case number were not always recorded and the list often contained as little information as the family's surname and the number of people in the family.

All of this meant not only that a lot of time spent working in the HPS systems was fruitless, but also that a substantial amount of time was spent visiting hotels which were supposed to have Travellers resident, only to discover on arrival that the family had moved on, in several cases months beforehand. In two cases, the hotel had no recall of the particular families ever having stayed there and yet, according to the HPS White Cards, they were still in residence.

Contacting the families in hotels
The next task was deciding the best way to contact people. I decided against writing to them because some Travellers neither read nor write, and decided against telephoning because I thought it would complicate matters unnecessarily to try and establish who I was over the telephone and I did not want to be confused with HPS staff. I decided the best thing would be to visit the people in hotels and ask if I could talk to them.

Having decided to do this I decided also, to save visiting hotels twice over, to interview both Travellers and Hotel Managers as I went along. In the event, however, hotels were usually visited more than once. This was necessary in order to meet with families, who often went out early in the morning and did not return until late in the evening.

The problems associated with visiting the hotels were several. First of all, I would have to turn up at hotel room doors and explain who I was and what I was doing, and also how I came to identify families as Travellers. I anticipated hostility on this count, because of the discrimination Travellers are used to suffering as a result of either identifying themselves, or being identified by others as Travellers. I prepared myself for rebuff on grounds that either people would say that they were not Travellers and therefore had no reason to talk to me, or on grounds that I had no business in coming to talk to them after having procured information about them without their consent or knowledge. If this were to happen I would not pursue the issue. Another problem with this approach was the sheer amount of travelling entailed and with no guarantee that I would be successful in interviewing anybody.

The idea of proceeding by hotel also threw up the whole issue of identifying people as Travellers to hotel managers, in terms of problems this might create for Travellers in hotels who had not previously been known by hotel management as such. The procedure I followed involved asking at reception for room numbers and presenting identification. After visiting the rooms I would then speak to the manager, explaining what the research was about. At this point clearly she or he will then realise that the people I wanted to see were Travellers. If that hotel discriminates against Travellers, and I identified certain people to management as Travellers, then this could expose these families to potential difficulties. This became clear after some weeks and I was not happy with this situation, particularly since it had been overwhelmingly the case that Travellers in hotels had experienced aggravation, from management and other residents, because of being Travellers.

As it happened, the issue of the project's lack of accountability to the Travelling community came to a head while these other questions were being discussed.

This meant that the interviews with Traveller families were done in two batches, first in August and the beginning of September 1987, and then in January and February 1988. Because of the problems involved with interviewing hotel managers and in the light of the pressure of time left in which to complete the project, the Steering Group decided, when the interviewing resumed in January, give lower priority to the interviewing of hotel managers. The approach to the families described here is the one used in both batches, with one exception. The interviewer employed near the end of the project often left messages for people to telephone her with a view to being interviewed because she was not able to contact them during the day.

The interview method

The research plan laid down that the researcher was to conduct in-depth interviews with Traveller families in HPS accommodation. A number of options were open here: I could construct a detailed questionnaire, ask the questions and fill in the answers, or I could construct a list of questions which would be less structured and leave more room for people to talk, if they wanted to, about concerns which might not be covered by the questions asked. I opted for the last method, as it was my aim to operate in a loosely structured way so that as full a picture as possible could be obtained from the people being interviewed.

A constant problem was finding people in. Most families preferred to leave the hotel after breakfast and stay out all day, only returning at night. Some families were staying in annexe flats belonging to the hotels, which meant that if they were not in, there was nobody to leave a message with. Despite this, 40 families were spoken to in all, which was a reasonably representative sample, given that, although there should have been at least 139 families in hotels in August/September, the number was in fact, as we shall see below substantially lower.

When it came to locating families a second time for interview in December 1987/January 1988, according to the White Card Index there should have been a total of 92 families in 39 hotels. The problems of this are discussed later.

This time, we decided to telephone the hotels first, to see if the families were still there, so as not to waste time visiting hotels in which people were no longer resident.

This telephone check revealed that there were only 35 Traveller families resident in 14 hotels, out of the 39 hotels we contacted. This illustrates the difficulty involved in estimating statistics, which will be looked at again later in this report.

This research project was based in the Central Race Relations Unit of the Council. When asking people to talk to us, we did not want to be confused with either the Travellers Outreach Worker or the HPS staff, so we had to try and explain to people that although we were 'from' the Council, we were not in a position of power regarding housing, site provision or anything else. Nevertheless, when it was possible, we tried to assist people with small practical problems like getting a message through to the HPS on their behalf when they could not get through on the telephone, or giving people contact numbers/addresses (eg for the Bayswater Project, Law Centre, Advice Agencies or Social Workers). We explained that this was not a residency check, and that we had no involvement with the DHSS, but that we were trying to find out people's experience of homelessness and what sort of service they received from

Camden HPS in order to write a report which just might improve the situation for Travellers. We explained that people were not obliged to talk to us at all and that whether they talked or not their chances of rehousing would not be affected.

The priority in conducting interviews was that people should feel at ease, and feel free to talk about anything linked to being homeless. Of equal importance was that they should feel free *not* to talk about any area. I did not want them to be confined by my perceptions of the situation, as demonstrated by the questions I asked.

I did not use a tape recorder because I felt it would inhibit conversation, and can be very threatening, especially as I was just turning up without warning, and the families did not know me, nor I them. Instead I wrote notes as we talked. This is not ideal but in the circumstances I felt it was the best thing to do. The other person conducting interviews operated in a similar way.

The following list of questions was used as a guideline in the interviews:

1. How long has the family been in HPS accommodation?
2. What is the size of the family?
3. When the family presented as homeless, how were they treated by HPS staff, and what problems did they encounter?
4. How is the family treated by hotel management?
5. Is there any experience of aggravation from other residents?
6. What has their experience in B&B been?
   — conditions in hotels, size, facilities, cleaning, including changing line, safety and fire, repairs, what floor is the family living on, access to cooking facilities, play/communal areas etc. Anything the family have experienced as a problem. Experience of homelessness.
7. Contact with agencies: is the family visited by anyone from Camden, or by Health Visitors etc?
8. Health Care issues: are there issues particularly affecting women and children living in hotels?
9. Is the family's presenting as homeless connected to lack of site provision and increased harassment under the Public Order Act, or connected to other issues? If so, what?
10. What is the family's ultimate goal?

4. Camden Homeless Persons Section

Off the road and into the system
Under Section 58(3) of the Housing Act (1985):

> "A person is homeless if he has accommodation but . . . (c) It consists of a moveable structure, vehicle or vessel designed or adapted for human habitation and there is no place where he is entitled or permitted both to place it and reside in it".

Of the 40 families we spoke to, 35 of them gave not being able to maintain the Travelling way of life because of the lack of permanent sites and acute shortage of stopping places in London, as their main reason for homelessness.

Time after time people spoke of how they could no longer face a life of being 'hounded and harassed' by the police or local authorities. Constant evictions taking place early in the morning with not even enough time to get some breakfast for the children, have made the Travelling way of life too hard. One woman said:

> "I can't face the pressure of moving all the time, especially with young children it's too risky now, and dangerous, with the police arresting people and having to pay big fines. I don't want my children to have to face the hardship I have been through, there is no life left in it . . ."

The other five families were made up of women on their own with children, who had become homeless because of the difficulties that face a woman travelling on her own, without members of her family for support. One of these was an older woman who felt she was not able, even with the support of her sons, to cope with the strain of travelling. She had travelled all her life, and found it very difficult to settle down. One of her biggest fears was that she would be re-housed in an area where she would be the

only Traveller, and have to cope with the hostility of people in houses towards Travellers.

Flowing from and caused by the squeeze being placed on the Travelling way of life were the other concerns that made people decide that they had no option but to move into housing.

Of these the one most often expressed was concern for the future of the children, particularly with regard to education.

Parents felt that the conditions of life on the road had a detrimental effect on their children. Since the introduction of the Public Order Act, police have been increasingly active and prompt about moving Travellers on, and arresting them. The continual strain and insecurity brought about by never being able to stop for long anywhere, affects the children, and leads to problems in the family.

Eighteen of the families we spoke to specifically said that the main concern for them was getting their children into school. On the road families could never stop anywhere long enough to allow their children to get a place in a school and settle down and benefit from the experience. Many parents felt that they had lost out through not having an education and did not want their children to have the same experience.

The general feeling was that the Travelling way of life is being restricted more and more and that this is pushing Travellers into houses. People spoke of being forced to settle down in order to give their children a chance in life. Some families said that they would rather travel if there were proper halting and permanent sites provided, but that they knew there was no chance of this so they had to do the best for their children.

Some of the families had made the decision that they had no future on the road after some particular setback had affected them, perhaps someone in the family became ill, or they experienced material hardship such as their trailer being lost through fire or some other circumstance. A few of the families had come over from Ireland with the intention of continuing to travel in London where they could earn their living. However, when they got here, they heard such horror stories from friends and relatives, mainly about their experiences at the hands of the police, that they did not even attempt to travel, knowing there was nothing in it for them and that it would only be a matter of time before they ended up homeless. One man had this to say:

"The travelling way of life is finished. In another few years all the Travellers will be in houses because there is nowhere else for them to go".

Having been forced to give up their traditional way of life the families had to find a way into the system for getting settled accommodation. They were therefore faced with having to deal with Camden's HPS.

It would be impossible to consider the issue of Travellers and Homelessness in Camden without taking a look at the way the Homeless Persons Section has perceived Travellers in the past. Travellers presenting as homeless in Camden have been constructed as, and come to be perceived as, a "problem".

The principal way this is achieved is by continually putting the spotlight on the ways in which the Travellers, by their presence, cause hiccups in a system which is hostile to their lifestyle and which has already been labouring under a burden of mismanagement over a long period. The focus therefore, is on the Travellers as "a problem" instead of being on the institution, in this case, Camden Council and its failure to take into account the particular housing needs of Travellers. Travellers are a particular group with legitimate housing needs, some of which flow directly from Camden's failure to provide even as much as one permanent site for Travellers in the Borough. As long as Travellers remain "the problem" the Council will not need to address its lack of service provision to this particular group.

A question of numbers?

When the "problem" of Travellers has been given an airing by the Housing Department, the numbers of Travellers presenting as homeless in Camden has been the jump-off point for the raising of alarm and suspicion. For instance, at the June 1986 meeting of the Travellers Officer Group, the Assistant Director of Housing (Needs) reported that "the number of Travelling families presenting as homeless had put a strain on resources. At present there are approximately 125 families in temporary accommodation". Singling out a group in terms of their numbers and linking them in this way to a strain on the resources of the HPS is a very dubious practice.

It would appear that the number of Travellers presenting as homeless is being quoted here for the purpose of laying the responsibility for a strain on HPS resources on the Travellers' presence.

Apart from the fact that singling out Travellers is a discriminatory practice, the question also has to be asked, how were the statistics quoted arrived at?

It is difficult to actually arrive at a statistic of this sort which bears any resemblance to reality, given the state of disarray in the HPS administrative systems at the time this research was carried out.

Possibly the figures quoted for the number of Travellers in emergency accommodation at various times, came straight out of the White Card Index, using the criteria to identify Travellers as distinct from others that have been used in this Research. If this is so, it is most likely that the figures are unreliable.

At the start of this Research, according to the White Card Index, there should have been 198 Traveller families who had been placed in emergency accommodation by Camden. That 198 broke down as follows after cross-checking with the non-residency file and the Day Book:

Families booked in Until Further Notice (UFN)	*139*
Unclear if booked UFN or for limited period	*17*
Booked for a specific number of weeks	*27*
Moved to Stage II	*3*
Cancellations	*12*
TOTAL	*198*

Taking simply the Until Further Notice category, according to the records in HPS then, there were at least 139 families booked into B&B hotels at the end of July 1987. Those families booked in Until Further Notice,

23

were those who had been accepted as priority homeless by Camden. It can be assumed from this that the families could reasonably be expected to be in hotels throughout August and beyond.

Between 3 August and 28 August, a sample 32 hotels were visited. There were 52 Traveller families in these hotels out of a total number of 79 homeless families altogether.

According to the records in HPS there should have been 78 Traveller families booked in Until Further Notice resident in these 32 hotels. So there were 26 Travellers families who apparently existed in HPS records but who were not in the hotels.

I have gone into detail here to illustrate how difficult it is to actually arrive at a definitive figure. The unreliability of the information gleaned from the White Card Index, the non-residence file in the day book, coupled with the continual movement of people in and out of hotels because of cancellations, decanting from one hotel to another, and moves either into permanent housing or out of the HPS system altogether, means that any figures taken out of the White Card Index are liable to be inaccurate. Clearly, one of the things that was happening was that families were being moved from one hotel to another and being counted in both places.

Another possibility is that the statistics quoted were arrived at by using the criteria of identifying Traveller families by their name and the size of the family and then simply counting from the hotels occupation list on this basis. This must be challenged, because it is arbitrary, and relies on, and reinforces stereotypes. It does not bear any credible relation to reality.

Either way, the statistics quoted must be seen as of no consequence as far as the issue of Travellers and Homelessness is concerned, except in a negative sense. This whole exercise must be seen as an attempt on the part of the Housing Department to turn the spotlight away from the failure of the Council to either address in a serious manner the urgent need for permanent sites in the Borough, or to employ resources via the Housing Department to attempt to meet the housing needs of Travellers presenting as homeless. Undoubtedly the crisis in HPS which is referred to in greater detail in Section 5 of this report was a major contributory factor to this situation being allowed to arise.

Approaching the issue in terms of numbers and resources, however, only serves to promote and legitimise anti-Traveller feeling, by linking the presence of Travellers to difficulties within the Homeless Persons Section.

24

It is interesting to note that although the Housing Department has been able consistently to produce 'statistics' in relation to the number of Traveller families presenting as homeless, they have been unable to produce statistics as to the number of families who were given travel warrants by Camden in the context of the recent row (which we discuss later) over the so-called "repatriation" policy. It is also worth noting that figures have not been produced as to the number of Traveller families that are being permanently rehoused. Could this be, because, according to their own records, out of a total of 731 homeless families rehoused in 1987, only 29 were Travellers?

Approaching Camden Homeless Persons Section (HPS)

Camden HPS has now reopened having been closed to the public for 10 months since April 1987.[6]

During this period, homeless people in priority need in Camden were obliged to telephone the HPS in order to get access to emergency accommodation. The telephone service only operated on weekday mornings which meant that anyone who was homeless outside these hours was left to fend for themselves.

Getting a reply from the emergency number was extremely difficult. One agency tried for two weeks to get through to the number with no success, and was forced as a result, to turn to neighbouring Boroughs for help in placing homeless families.

Ten of the families we spoke to had become homeless after April 1987. All had difficulty trying to get through to the HPS emergency number. Six of the families could not get through at all.

In the end, two of them turned to the Irish Centre for help and were referred in this way. Another went to the door of Instrument House, where the HPS was based, and, after some time spoke to a member of staff who told them to go back to the telephone box and try again and this time he would be waiting for the call. In this way they finally did get accommodated.

Three other families made contact through the Camden Travellers Outreach Worker, who only managed to get through on an internal line.

Of the remaining four families, two spent a whole day in the Housing Department but eventually managed to make contact, while another spent three days trying to get through, during which time they had to stay with friends on an unofficial site, squashed into a small caravan.

The last family, a woman on her own with small children, spent two days trying before making contact. Having got through to the number she was told to 'hold on' for long periods and had to not only keep putting money in the box at peak time, but also had to cope with the abuse from the inevitable queue of people waiting to use the box. Add to this, two or three small children and it's little wonder that people feel they are being punished for being homeless in the first place. This woman had fled domestic violence, and recounted her shame and embarrassment at having to discuss the circumstances that led to her being homeless over the telephone with a stranger, from a public place, with other people listening.

Another woman described how, after giving her details, she was told she would be called back on that number, as soon as a hotel had been found for her to stay in that night. After one and a half hours of waiting by the public box, and suffering torment every time someone used it in case HPS would not be able to get through to her, she tried to telephone them but to no avail.

By now she could no longer wait as she had to pick up her children from a friend who was looking after them. The next day she had to start again from scratch.

With one exception, we were only able to speak to Travellers who were successful in securing emergency accommodation through HPS. People who were turned away over the telephone remain for the most part, unrecorded and invisible. One young Traveller woman did however describe her experience to us. The following is her account of what happened. Thrown out of her home in Ireland because she was pregnant she travelled on the night boat, and she ended up on the streets of Euston, where a policeman directed her to the Town Hall. Here she was given the Homeless Persons Service emergency number. It was a Friday morning. At 12 o'clock she got through to the Assistant Director of Housing.

She told him her story, that she had nowhere to go that night, and that her father had beaten her and thrown her out because she was pregnant. Asked if she had proof that she was pregnant, she said "no". In that case, she was told, nothing could be done to assist her. She pleaded that she had nowhere to go, knew nobody, and would have to stay on the street. The reply to this was that there were many young girls in her situation in London, and nothing could be done for her without proof of pregnancy. She told us that as a young woman, alone in a strange city, she was offered no advice or sympathy. Neither was it suggested to her that if she got proof of pregnancy she could come back to the HPS and accommodation would be found for her.

She ended up walking around Kings Cross, with no support, until she was directed to a local voluntary organisation who managed to find her accommodation for one night in an emergency hotel.

The other 30 families we contacted had approached the HPS when it was open.

Some of them had waited all day to see somebody, but with two exceptions they all said HPS staff had been very helpful to them.

In the case of the exceptions, the people felt that because they were Travellers they were being treated sharply and given unnecessary trouble. One woman said:

". . . because we're Travellers, they think we're ignorant, but we shouldn't be treated any different to anyone else".

Both families felt they had been insulted by the HPS staff who had seen them, and felt that they had been kept waiting longer than other people because the staff member in question "did not like Travellers".

Here it is important to distinguish between individual and institutional responses. Face to face contact between Travellers and HPS staff appears to have been on the whole good, but Camden's structure ensures that individual contacts are kept to a minimum and thereafter the institution takes over, providing much greater opportunities for discrimination and alienation.

Time and again the experience of Travellers approaching HPS highlight the problem of lack of contact with the providers of the service. Once through the hurdle of booking into temporary accommodation all contact with HPS ceases, with the exception of the occasional letter or abrupt cancellation of accommodation. Travellers only relationship is with hotel management who are at best indifferent and at worst hostile.

Not surprisingly, in this situation there was widespread misunderstanding of the re-housing procedure and many thought they would be given a choice of being re-housed in Camden or elsewhere in London, when most of them will in fact be given an offer outside of Camden under the London Area Mobility Scheme.

One family said they had been given a map and a letter but did not understand it and could not make contact with Camden because of the restricted service.

Another family said they had been offered a tenancy but the offer had been withdrawn because the Council said the flat was too small. The family were left not knowing what would happen next or what stage their case was at.

Others had been moved from one hotel to another for no apparent reason, and did not understand what was going on. This sort of experience serves to add to the insecurities faced by families living in hotels, who feel forgotten about and isolated and who, in the case of Camden during the course of this project, were unable to even make contact with the HPS to enquire about their housing situation.

This lack of contact and monitoring of individual cases leaves them vulnerable, isolated and unsupported and in turn gives hoteliers carte-blanche to behave towards Travellers as they wish, secure in the knowledge that the Council will be in no position to challenge discriminatory treatment.

Relations with hotel management

The average time the families we contacted had been living in B&B was 11 months. Some had been living in various hotels for as long as two years and some were in their first weeks of hotel life.

The most recurring problem for the people we spoke to was that of being on the receiving end of discriminatory treatment from hotel management.

As well as trouble with hotel management and other residents who blamed the Travellers for any irregularity in the hotel, the families had to cope with a new lifestyle unlike anything they had experienced before. Hotel accommodation for homeless families is a dire response to an escalating need which shows no sign of abating. Living in a hotel brings with it a whole string of stresses and difficulties which affect every part of a person's life. For Travellers particularly the restraints of this life are severe, being used to a life largely spent outdoors and independent of settled society.

Originally, part of this project time was to be spent interviewing hotel managers about their understanding, experience of, and attitude towards Travellers. Because of the problems associated with this, which have already been outlined, it was discontinued, but not before 11 hotel managers had been spoken to.

The questions used were as follows:

— In your experience, do Travellers have special needs?
— When Camden HPS place families in your hotel, do they ever identify families over the telephone as being Travellers?
— What is your policy/practice about accepting or not accepting Traveller families?
— What has been your experience with Travellers in the hotel?

It soon became clear that hotel managers' understanding of Travellers in common with the rest of the settled population was one which grew out of a set of negative assumptions. They usually made a distinction between Traveller families in general and those currently staying in their hotel who they referred to as being "all right". This distinction usually came at the end of the interview. Beforehand, they spoke about Travellers in a way that inferred that all Travellers were the same, (the same tending to mean destructive and troublesome). They said they would "not really" want any more Travellers in the hotel, but that they would give everybody a fair chance of a week's trial, and take it from there.

It is Camden's policy to withdraw from a hotel if that hotel refuses to take any family. Despite this some hotels which did have Camden families resident, stated categorically that they would not accept Traveller families, and some no longer had Traveller families resident.

One hotel manager told how she had refused to have one Camden family upon hearing their name over the telephone, a name which indicated to her that they could be Travellers. On this occasion, instead of HPS withdrawing or even threatening to withdraw from the hotel as is supposed to be their policy, or even challenging the hotelier, the HPS staff member persuaded the manager to take the family, by saying that they "looked reasonable enough". This was in response to the hotelier asking about the family's appearance.

If behaviour of this sort is taking place it indicates that some HPS staff may be colluding with the prejudices of certain hotel managers and not implementing their own policies. This has very serious implications in terms of the service Camden HPS offers to Travellers.

There is little point in adopting policies which remain on paper. If individual members of staff tolerate discrimination simply to get the job done, this is a fault of the management of the Homeless Persons Service. If an institution is serious in its intent to eliminate discrimination from its service provision a management led policy is essential. In fact, however this whole area of Camden's relationship with hoteliers, in terms of policy implementation with regard to how hoteliers treat homeless families is both problematic and ambiguous.

Conditions for homeless people in hotels are as "good or bad as the management", according to the HPS hotels officer. Camden does not have a contract with hotels, but simply pays for accommodation for the families in the same way as anybody booking into a hotel pays their bills. This means that in effect, the only control Camden has over the way their clients are treated is to either apply 'subtle pressure' such as appeals to reason and conscience, or to withdraw from the hotel.[7] Withdrawing from hotels may eliminate one problem but it also presents a whole set of other problems, because new hotels have to be found, families 'decanted' from one hotel to another and the whole operation would cause a lot of disruption both for the families concerned and for the HPS.

In July 1987 Camden HPS drew up procedures for staff to follow regarding moves between hotels and non-residence. According to these, a hotelier may change a family's booking for a number of reasons, among which are the following:

"B. 4. Unacceptable behaviour of family. In this case the Senior Adviser will decide whether or not, alternative temporary accommodation should be provided.

In the following instances a family should be told that no more hotel accommodation will be provided.
  i) racial harassment
  ii) sexual harassment
  iii) Where client has been violent to other residents or hotel staff or has been threatening or abusive. (Cancellation should follow investigation or reports from reliable sources eg council officers or the police.)
  iv) client has caused serious damage to property."

This procedure represents a major hurdle for Travellers in B&B because it places the word of the client against that of the hotelier and possibly, the police.

Given that HPS have acknowledged in the past the difficulty in getting a number of hotels to accept Traveller families, and that Camden's policy is that they must accept them or lose Camden's custom, it would make sense for a hotelier not wanting to accept Travellers but also not wanting Camden to pull out altogether from his hotel, to initially accept those families and then find a way of ensuring that their stay in his hotel is as short as possible, without him falling from grace with the HPS. Clause B.4 is wide open to being used by hoteliers in such a discriminatory way. "Unacceptable behaviour" is a vague term, and on the strength of a hotel manager's word, a homeless family may be shunted from one hotel to another, or worse, may have their B&B cancelled completely, although in this case the word of the hotelier alone is not enough.

The police may be considered 'a reliable source' by HPS for determining whether a client has been threatening or abusive, but in the case of Travellers, it would not be unreasonable to expect that the police will take a less than favourable view of any sort of disruption with which Travellers are linked.

One family we spoke to told of how they had become involved in an argument with a member of staff in a hotel, after discovering that he had been making sexual advances to their 13 year old daughter. The father was understandably, very upset and was shouting.

The police were called by management, and the father was warned that he was close to being arrested. Nothing was said to the staff member. The mother calmed her husband down, and they went to their room, collected their belongings and left the hotel. After this they tried to get a place on a site in Camden, but before long, were homeless again and forced to re-approach the HPS, who booked them into another hotel.

Had the family not left of their own volition, it is conceivable that they would have been cancelled anyway, and no doubt the police would have been able to confirm that the client had been "threatening and abusive". In this case, it did not happen, but it can be argued that it is far from being beyond possibility that in a situation of this sort Travellers will not get a fair hearing.

This incident is an example of the damage done by piecemeal policy making. Our research has shown how hard it is to identify a comprehensive policy in HPS which provides a balance between the needs of homeless people as the consumers and those of the Council and hoteliers as providers of a service. In situations such as the one described above the family should have had the support of the Council (which has after all, specific policies to combat sexual harassment), instead they felt no one would believe their account of the incident and so they had no way of seeking redress.

Several of the people we spoke to complained that they were blamed for any damage that was done in the hotel, regardless of whether or not there was proof. On the strength of this, some families had been moved to another hotel and warned about "their behaviour".

I asked HPS staff about how this procedure works, and it was confirmed that often a family are moved on the strength of a telephone call from the hotelier, claiming the family have caused damage in the hotel.

According to the procedure, clients should be informed of their position verbally and in writing, if their booking is cancelled. One family we spoke to had been moved from one hotel to another very quickly, and had no idea as to why this had happened.

In October 1987, solicitor Trevor Asserson challenged Camden Council in the High Court on behalf of a homeless family with six children who had been evicted from their B&B hotel because the hotelier alleged that the children had broken a water pipe, flooding the premises. The family were Travellers. According to their solicitor the Assistant Director of Housing (Needs) in Camden refused to accommodate the family because:

> *"On the basis of a telephone call to the hotel he assumed that the children had caused the damage and that the family were intentionally homeless".* (Ham and High *30.10.87.*)

The High Court ordered Camden to rehouse the family immediately and set a hearing for 26 October. On 25 October the Council contacted the solicitor and admitted it was in the wrong.

> *"It admitted that it should not have refused to house the family and on that basis we settled the action".* Trevor Asserson (Irish Post *14.11.87.*)

Camden are in a difficult position in terms of ensuring that their clients are treated properly by hoteliers, because hotels are not part of the Council, and so are not bound by the Council's rules and policies.

What Camden are entitled to do, however, is to make sure that their clients are receiving the service being paid for.

Conditions in temporary accommodation

Of the families we interviewed some lived in hotels while others were living in properties belonging to and managed by the hotel, known as annexes. These were usually flats or in one or two cases, houses. They count as B&B accommodation but the landlords do not have to supply breakfast. This is because if food is provided in these units, there are then grounds for Environmental Health and Planning to claim a change of use of the premises and this causes problems. Three of the families were living in Stage II accommodation.

Camden's Environmental Health Department inspect hotels and flats to approve them before Camden moves families in, and after that, inspections are carried out every three months. The environmental health officer involved with this work acknowledged that many of the hotels Camden uses are not up to standard, because of the difficulties associated with finding suitable hotels, or getting hotels to co-operate with the Council in providing the facilities required.

Camden has only one hotels officer, who is supposed to be responsible for practically anything to do with hotels, from finding hotels suitable for

Camden to use, to liaising with hotel managers and residents in order to ensure that things are running smoothly. Clearly, one post is not enough to cover such a wide area of work.

Annexe flats/houses

Many of the families living in the annexe flats were relieved to be out of the hotel, because in the flats they felt they had a place which offered more space and better facilities, and being away from the hotel meant that they did not have to try to keep their children occupied in one or two rooms, or eat out all the time, or cope with the strain of sharing cooking and washing facilities with strangers. They also felt the flats were safer for their children, because especially in the bigger hotels, families had experienced instances of attempted and actual sexual abuse and assault of their children from other people resident in the hotel, as well as from staff members or unknown persons. Living in the annexes also meant that friends and extended family could come freely to visit, something which was not always possible in hotels. Some annexes have gardens and this is also a plus.

On the other hand, living in the flats can be very isolating, especially if they are far away from any friends or relatives.

Although conditions in the flats we visited were usually decent, there were some instances where families believed they had been given poor treatment by the hotel because of being Travellers. One family had a broken cooker in their flat. They asked the hotel to repair it, but nothing happened, so after one month of waiting, they bought a second hand cooker themselves because they would have had nothing to cook on otherwise.

Another family's cooker had 'blown up', and was unusable. They had been waiting one week for it to be repaired. Other complaints were about flats being dirty when the family moved in and of there not being enough, or only very poor quality furniture in them. When one family had complained to the hotel about the condition of their flat, they had been told it would do them because they did not deserve anything better.

One family had been three weeks in their accommodation when we spoke to them. They had two flats, in which the furniture consisted of beds, one wardrobe, one table and five chairs altogether. The flats were newly decorated and carpeted throughout and had an intercom system. The kitchen was fitted but had no fridge. There were two bedrooms. This was for a family of nine.

One bedroom in each flat had a fitted cupboard, and one of the flats had a lot of damp with fungus growing on the wall and inside the cupboard, where the family's clothes and shoes were covered in mould.

The flats were on the second and third floors of large houses with five flats altogether in the building, including the basement.

The day we visited, the mother told us that she was terrified of being evicted and at first thought that was what we had come for. This was because another Travelling family had been evicted from the flats a few days before, on the grounds that they had written on walls in the house, near the communal telephone.

The family described how "a man" had come and told the family in question that they had five minutes to leave, and had shouted and sworn at them in an abusive manner. He also shouted at the family we interviewed who were nearby when all this was going on. He said they had been given good flats to live in and had made a mess of them and he threatened to evict them too if they 'stepped out of line'.

After evicting the first family, he accused the children of the other family of having knocked bricks from a wall in the rear garden, and said they could not go into the garden any more. The parents had tried to keep the children indoors in case of any more trouble. When we visited, they were all in one room with their mother, sitting around the floor as there were not enough chairs to sit on.

He had also accused the children of having soiled carpet on the stairs, and in the bedrooms. The mother showed me the stains, which in the bedrooms, were the result of a rusty iron bedstead resting on damp carpet, and on the stairs, the result of leakage from a fire extinguisher.

One of the children, after being shouted at by 'the man', had a severe asthma attack, and her mother was anxious and frightened in case she suffered any more.

The family's flats were spotless, but this did not stop the mother from worrying about cleaning them. No hoover or other utensils had been provided to the family, who had cleaned the carpets by hand.

On the morning of the day we called, a woman had arrived while the family were cleaning the stairs and told them that she had now been employed as a cleaner. This was the first time anybody had come to clean the house. The family were also told however that the Environmental Health Department were coming in a few days.

When the family asked the hotel about more furniture, "the man" told them that it was up to them to apply to the DHSS for a furniture grant! The family did not know what they were entitled to, and because the owner had threatened them with eviction they were too intimidated to ask any more questions.

Upon enquiry, it transpired that the family were being short-changed by the hotel, and that nobody from the Council had yet been to inspect the accommodation to make sure that it was up to standard. Families in annex flats/houses, are supposed to be provided with beds, chest of drawers, wardrobes, table and chairs, cooker, fridge, kitchen equipment and seating. It is not up to the clients to procure furniture from the DHSS. The hotel is supposed to provide cleaning and change of linen once a week, as well as general management. As a result of this incident the Hotels Officer sent a letter to hoteliers, reminding them of this.

Several of the families we contacted who lived in annexes had found that their presence was objected to by their neighbours, who blamed the Travellers for any misdemeanor in the locality.

One family had been refused service in shops and another had been severely harassed by the police who told the local shopkeepers to beware of the family because they were Travellers. At 5am one morning, the police raided the Traveller family's flat, ransacking it. They even searched the pockets of the children's clothes, and took away the family's hi-fi and TV, as well as arresting the mother and her teenage son. At no time did they tell the family why all this was going on. The mother and son spent all day from 5am-5pm in the police station, during which time they did not get as much as a drink. When they asked for a cup of water, it was thrown at them to the great amusement of the officers present. When they were released at 5pm, they were given back their TV and hi-fi. The police said that they "had reason to suspect" that the family had stolen the goods as there had been a spate of robberies committed in the district. This family said that being in a house made them more vulnerable to being harassed in this way. If they had not got a receipt for all the goods they owned, then the police would have assumed they were stolen. As they were the only Traveller family in the area they felt isolated, and were angered by the fact that they were being subjected to such overt anti-Traveller behaviour, even though they had done nothing to deserve it.

Another family in a similar situation told how their children had been blamed for a mugging even though the oldest was only five years old.

This family wanted to settle down in permanent accommodation but their experiences at the hands of house-dwellers have been such that they suspect that they will not be able to stay anywhere for long because anti-Traveller feeling and activity among house-dwellers will force them out of their home.

35

These experiences are included at length here because they serve to illustrate the problems which occur when the recipients of a council service are so isolated from the providers of that service. All contact with the council ceases, once families are placed in accommodation, and Travellers become subject to a constant round of intimidation and harassment, some of it minor but some of it far more serious.

Bed and Breakfast Hotels

In terms of conditions in B&B hotels, in the case of the families the main pressures came from the following areas:

— lack of safety
— lack of space and facilities
— isolation
— poor diet and health problems

These areas overlap all the time and are inter-connected, as well as being compounded in some cases by aggressive management in the hotel, and conditions in B&B related to using substandard hotels.

In August 1987 a Traveller child fell to his death from the fourth floor balcony of an HPS hotel. We visited the hotel which had a large number of Traveller families resident. Just after the accident, when we spoke to some of the families, they said they had been asking the management three weeks prior to the accident, to secure the balcony windows from which the child fell. After the child's death Camden officers discovered five inch gaps between the hotel wall and the balcony railings and faulty locks on the balcony doors. They ordered that work should begin immediately to close the gaps and fix the locks.

At the time of our visit, the hotel was being refurbished and Camden was moving its families to another hotel. The families we spoke to said that management were very slow to do repairs in the hotel and that there had been an instance of a man coming into the bedroom of two young girls at night because the door locks were broken, and threatening them. They complained that at the height of the summer season they had been made to sleep four to a room with only two single beds, so that the hotel could accommodate tourists, and they also complained that the rooms were full of cockroaches, which ran over their beds at night.

Those families who had witnessed the accident were terrified that something similar would happen to their children. One woman was so anxious that she refused to let her child out of her sight.

36

This was the fourth known death of a child living in B&B accommodation.

Raising children in a bed and breakfast hotel means worrying continually about their safety. Hotels were not built with the accommodation of children for long periods, in mind. Some of the hazards we came across in various hotels used by Camden were faulty fire extinguishers or none at all; broken latches or doors; rubbish lying in corridors; windows left wide open with no safety catches or slats; broken light bulbs which left whole corridors either in darkness or dimly lit; kitchens with cookers that did not work; fire exits locked with no key in sight or fire exits open for ventilation and leaving easy access to roof tops with no railings or protection. Some hotels did not have a fire escape at all and when we followed directions to the fire exits in one hotel, we went around an elaborate circle only to arrive back where we started.

The fire exits in another hotel were locked with no key and blocked by bags of rubbish. Two doors which were marked "fire exit" actually led into two rooms occupied by families, and the "fire exit" was out through the front windows into a basement yard.

As well as worries about the physical safety of children in hotels, many parents we spoke to were concerned about the psychological effect on their children of living in a hotel. Not only had there been cases of actual and potential sexual abuse of children but also parents were worried about the sorts of behaviour the children were exposed to, such as soliciting, drug abuse and violence especially in hotels in the Central London Area.

Getting children into school is a problem for homeless families, who often have to wait months for a place in a school. Being moved from one hotel to another, as most of the families we spoke to had been, means that having got children settled into school, they often have to be taken out again and wait in the new area for a school place. One family we spoke to told how when they approached the local school about getting places for the children, they had been refused on grounds that the hotel did not constitute a "proper address". Even finding out how to apply for a school place is a challenge for some families, especially those new to the country and not familiar with the system. The same upheaval is involved when taking children out of nurseries, playgroups or creches, and this has a very unsettling effect on the whole family.

Camden Recreation Department do have a Homeless Families Playteam who are providing an essential service to families living in emergency accommodation.

The team have provided playschemes and over 5s facilities in some of the larger hotels used by Camden, as well as running projects during school holidays such as day trips to the seaside, video projects, photography, music and dancing, and visits to other projects. The team have also worked with families in Stage II accommodation, and as well as working with young people, have provided weight-training sessions for adults, activities for women in co-operation with the Mary Ward Centre and some facilities for the elderly.

This service eases some of the burden on some families, providing an opportunity for children to play and develop in a safe space, and giving parents a break from the constant strain of occupying their children's attention and providing an outlet for their energy. A number of the families we spoke to spend their days away from the hotel, often with other Travellers on sites around London. In this, their children are fortunate, they are not as damaged as they could be by a prolonged stay in inadequate accommodation.

Lack of cooking facilities in hotels is a major problem. Often a family may be living on the top floor, while the kitchen is in the basement. If there is no place to eat downstairs, then food has to be carried back to the room. Most of the women we spoke to who were faced with such conditions, found that it was an ordeal to provide a meal for their family. Not only did they have to get access to a cooker, but they also had to watch their children while cooking to make sure they did not get injured or scalded. Having managed to cook the food, it then had to be carried up several flights of stairs to their room to be eaten. As well as the danger of burns and scolds from carrying hot food upstairs and trying to watch toddlers at the same time, the women found that by the time they had gone through this ritual, the food was cold and unappetising.

As a result many families tended to eat take-away food or eat in cafes. As well as stretching their income, this also resulted in an unhealthy diet of mainly chips and hamburgers and other fried foods to which the families attributed stomach upsets and ulcers, which were common among the families we spoke to.

Some women felt that skin problems like eczema and psoriasis were related to the stresses involved in living in hotels, as they had only experienced some of those complaints since being homeless. Other health complaints were migraine headaches, backache, and nervous rashes. A number of the women we interviewed, described their situation in terms of "living on their nerves", and were using tranquilizers regularly.

Both men and women said that stress often manifested itself in tensions within the family and many couples said they got irritated more easily with the children and each other since living in B&B. Depression was common among the women, as a result of living in overcrowded conditions, and worrying constantly about their family's well-being. One young woman suffered from severe depression and had attempted suicide on a number of occasions. Frequently, living in hotels was likened to being imprisoned, and in cases where there was only one Traveller family in a hotel, isolation added to the strain.

Some of the women we spoke to had babies, but had no cot for them. They also had no means of heating the baby's bottle at night. Carrying children, shopping and prams up and down several flights of stairs made some of the women feel very tired, especially those with young babies. One family had no chairs in their rooms and had to sit on the beds. The woman had had two caesarean sections and found sitting without the support of a chair gave her constant backache.

Several families had no fridge in their room and had to leave food out on the windowsill. Because a number of hotels were in the Bayswater area, families found shops were expensive and not geared to providing basic food stuffs. This meant travelling some distance to do shopping, and with no place to store food, this had to be done several times a week.

The only people who ever seemed to visit the families we spoke to were health visitors. Some families had problems getting registered with a GP and did not know where to turn for help and advice with welfare benefits problems, and problems about getting children into school.

Stage II

Stage II property is temporary accommodation owned or leased by Camden which is used to house homeless families while they are waiting to be permanently accommodated by the Council.

The standard of Stage II properties varies widely, some being above permanent Council housing standard and some below. If a family does not like the accommodation offered or its location, this is not accepted as a reason for refusing to take up residency. If a family do not occupy the temporary accommodation offered to them, they will be obliged to make their own temporary housing arrangements.

Usually a family is moved into Stage II after having spent a period of time in a B&B hotel. Households with no local connection in Camden or any other UK authority will generally not be placed in Stage II.

Three of the families we interviewed were in Stage II accommodation. One family were living in a small block of flats owned by Camden in the NW1 area. They moved in after having spent eight months in hotels.

The flat had two bedrooms, a living room, bathroom and small kitchen. It was clean and in good decorative order, being well heated. The family were overcrowded, because they have two boys and one girl, which meant the parents had to sleep in the living room on a bed settee.

The family were notified on a Friday that they had to move the following Monday from the hotel to the flat. This was not enough time to make arrangements for the move, which was done by taxi, as they had no other transport. They had not been informed by the Council that they could be helped with the move until they had already moved, by which time it was too late. The family were angered about this sort of carelessness which had cost them a lot.

The family were living on the eighth floor of the block, which had two lifts and one staircase. The lifts were often broken, as they were the day we visited, which meant using the stairs, which were poorly lit, with several bulbs being broken, and blocked by bags of rubbish and dumped household effects. Inside the front door of the building was a reception hatch. The family, who were six weeks in the flats, had only ever seen it open once, and then only for half an hour. There was nobody to ask advice from or to liaise with regarding problems that may crop up in the flats. Post delivery caused a lot of difficulty.

Before Christmas the family's giro went missing. Apparently the postman is not allowed to deliver mail through the flat doors for 'security reasons' — this is what the Council told the family when they enquired. This means the post is delivered into the front hall and left lying there for people to pick it up. Whoever arrives in the hall first, has access to everyone's mail, and there have been allegations of mail being opened and stolen from the front hall. People have no way of knowing whether or not post arrives. One day, the man of the family went down to get the post and was asked by the postman to sign for a letter. When he pointed out that it was not for him the postman said 'oh, just sign it'. This is a worry to the family, as anyone can sign for anybody else's mail.

When they tried to contact Camden about this they were continually put through to people who did not know what they were talking about, so in the end, through sheer frustration, they gave up trying to make contact.

The other two families were living in flats in a run down block belonging to Camden also in the NW1 area. These had no heating except for an open fire or electric fire in the living room. Initially one of the families had been on the fourth floor but had asked to be moved because it was too dangerous for the children, and had then been given a flat on the ground floor. The flat was very cold and poorly furnished. The family complained of being harassed by other residents because they were Travellers. They did not understand the rehousing procedure, had had no contact with HPS for some time, and were unable to get through on the telephone. They preferred the flat to the hotel because it gave the children some room to play, and they had a bit of privacy. They had been 14 months in emergency accommodation.

The other family a woman and her two children, one male and one female, were placed in different B&B hotels and then in Stage II accommodation.

The flat the family have been living in has got two bedrooms, one living room and a kitchen. There is no bathroom, the bath being in the kitchen. The only form of heating is an electric heater in the living room and the water is also heated by electricity which means large bills. The family described the accommodation as 'freezing and full of cockroaches'. Despite these conditions they did not complain, except on one count — they wondered why they had seen other Camden families rehoused from Levita House, families who had not been there as long as they had. They tried to make enquiries about their case but were unable to talk to anyone in HPS because it was closed and they could not get through on the telephone. As we had a way of contacting HPS, we agreed to make enquiries on their behalf.

It transpired that their case had been "accidentally" closed. The Advisor who had been dealing with this family had since moved out of Camden and the file stated that the family had "not been around since 9.4.87". No evidence was given to back up this claim; nobody was recorded as having visited the family, who said they had never received a visit from anybody from Camden. As a result of the enquiry, the case has been re-opened and the family will now be given one offer in Camden. If they refuse this offer for any reason, then the Council will have discharged its duty and no longer be responsible for the family. Had HPS not been contacted about this family, they would probably have remained indefinitely in their present accommodation, forgotten about.

5. Camden policy — a policy of non-harassment?

Camden is an inner London Borough with a sizeable Travelling Community. Despite the fact that it is more than 20 years since the Caravan Sites Act (1968) became law, Camden still has not provided one permanent site for Travellers.

Camden sought designation claiming it had no land available for a Travellers site and received designation under the Act with nil provision in 1981.

Adopting the policy — key features

Up until May 1984 the Council had generally adopted the practice of evicting Travellers off its land as soon as possible. In May 1984 the Council adopted a non-harassment policy towards Travellers and agreed that using its designation powers would be discriminatory. The key features of the non-harassment policy are as follows:

1. The Council will not seek to evict Travellers from its own land until such time as the land is required urgently for other uses.
2. All Council Departments are asked to endorse a non-harassment policy towards Travellers and to ensure that they are not acting in a discriminatory way towards Travellers.
3. The provision of permanent and temporary sites in Camden.
4. The Council will not use its 'designation' powers under the Caravan Sites Act (1968) except in exceptional circumstances.

How it was supposed to work

Under the non-harassment policy, when Travellers occupy Council owned land in Camden and if the land is not urgently required for other uses, they should be allowed to stay, and arrangements should be made for temporary use as an "unofficial" Travellers Site. The Council should

Temporary unofficial site at Kings Cross

ensure provision of fresh water, toilet facilities and refuse collection. If the occupied land is required urgently for other uses or is maintained for amenity use eg public open space, the Council will seek repossession through the Courts, but only on the authority of a Chair's Action and after a full report has been made by Council officers, including the Assistant Chief Executive (Race). Until such time as eviction takes place, facilities should be provided on site where possible.

Within the Council there exists a Travellers Officers Group, which meets regularly with Travellers representatives to discuss and monitor the implementation of the non-harassment policy. One post in the council, that of a Travellers Outreach Worker, exists to co-ordinate and develop the Council's policy, and to liaise between the Council and the Travelling community. When the Council adopted the non-harassment policy in 1984, it said that this policy was a sensible way of resolving a difficult situation. It also said that it would lead to better conditions both for Travellers and local residents, and that it would be an impetus for the provision of permanent sites within the Borough. It was also argued that by providing on-site facilities the risk of health hazards for the Travellers would be lessened, as well as the cost of clearing a site after an occupation, which would be to the ratepayers advantage. Allowing Travellers to stay

43

on "unofficial" sites would further mean that they would have better access to education. The policy was realistic in that it recognised that whether or not the Council provide facilities, Travellers would continue to occupy land in Camden and it sought to reduce nuisance and cost to the ratepayer as well as attempting to ensure that Travellers would get a better deal from local services and facilities.

However there proved to be a number of serious problems with the implementation of the policy.

What actually happened

What must have been one of the first applications of the policy in September 1984 immediately caused a major split amongst Labour councillors. Travellers moved onto the courtyard of Levita House part of a council estate and the Somers Town ward Councillors Tom Devine and Graham Shurety threatened not to back the non-harassment policy if sites such as Levita House were not excluded. They called for the immediate eviction of the Travellers and, according to press reports of the Race and community Relations Committee (21st August, 1984), (a) Councillor Tom Devine publicly distinguished between ordinary, decent people, ie tenants, and Travellers.

At the Race and Community Relations Committee of 19th November 1985 all four sites which had been identified and noted as possible permanent sites were rejected, and officers were requested to look for other sites and report back to the committee in six months time, after the forthcoming council elections in May.

Among the critics of the policy at the time was Tory councillor Ian Pasley-Tyler who accused the council of "mothballing this plan until after the elections — because you know it is political dynamite" (b). Councillor Barbara Beck, Chair of Race and Community Relations Committee at the time, admitted that there was a "lack of political will" for the provision of a permanent site in the borough (c). The same press report quoted councillors as being privately worried that a Travellers site could boost Alliance votes at the election (c). This occurred slightly more than one year after the adoption of the policy.

(a)   Ham and High 1.9.84 and Camden New Journal 1.9.84
(b)   *Camden chronicle* 20.12.85
(c)   *Camden New Journal* 20.12.85

However arguably one of the most vigorous attacks on the policy at that time came from within the party, from a newly selected candidate for the council's elections, Gareth Smyth, at that time secretary of Peckwater Estate Tenants Association. Mr Smyth issued a press statement accusing Travellers' children of running amok, causing great discomfort to tenants and Travellers and of, among other things, filling rubbish chutes with human excrement and stealing milk bottles (d). The stated purpose of this use of the press was to pressurise the council to encourage the landowners of the nearby Islip Street site, (British Rail), to evict the Travellers (e). British Rail won eviction orders on 14.1.86 (f). Since the application for the eviction was well under way in December 1985 what was the purpose of the publicity — an eviction or an appeal to racist views for votes? By January 1986 the Council Leader Phil Turner was publicly accusing his colleagues of hypocrisy saying "Local ward councillors say they are all for a site, but then say 'not in my ward'" (g). Again, by the end of 1986 the split between some newly elected councillors, including Gareth Smyth and Ken Hulme, and the Labour leadership had deepened with these councillors calling for ward councillors, to have powers of decision on evictions and for the use of the criminal rather than civil process to evict travellers (h). However Ken Hulme was able to say in December 1986 "Our policy on travellers is a disaster. We have failed to establish a permanent site and turned thousands off the idea" (h). So the split within Labour, though existing, could be exaggerated in its importance, because the central plank of the policy (ie provision of permanent sites) had never been implemented. Not only had no permanent sites been developed but at this time out of six council owned travellers' sites the council were planning to evict the occupants from five (i). Therefore it came as no surprise in January 1987 when the non-harassment policy was watered down with the addition of "nuisance criteria'.

Adding 'nuisance' criteria

The following criteria have been adopted for nuisance to be sufficient to warrant possession of a Travellers site:

(d) *Camden New Journal* 20.12.85.
(e) *Camden Chronicle* 20.12.85.
(f) *Ham & High* 31.1.86.
(g) *Camden New Journal* 30.1.86.
(h) *Camden New Journal* 11.12.86.
(i) *Ham & High* 19.12.86

1. Tipping by occupants on the site.
2. Intentional damage of Council facilities on the site or neighbouring properties after the occupation has occurred.
3. Immediate and serious risk to health and safety of Travellers or local residents.
4. Serious and uncontrollable noise or smoke nuisance.

The Council also agreed that

> *"No decision to evict Travellers from a site which is not immediately required will be taken without proper or due consideration being given to a report by the Assistant Chief Executive (Race) on the conditions likely to be faced by evicted Travellers in respect of the type of site they may go to: whether their children will be able to continue, or begin, proper schooling, and whether there will be adequate health care".*

Council officers were issued with guidelines on how to interpret and operate the nuisance criteria, and it was agreed that the criteria including the undertaking not to evict Travellers without due consideration to the position they faced, would be implemented with the concurrence of the Chair of the relevant Committee[8] on whose land the Travellers were and the Chair of the Race and Community Relations Committee, and after those Chairs have given due consideration to the views of elected Members from the appropriate wards.

The guidelines for implementation of the Nuisance Criteria, point out that it is important to recognise that complaints about occupations by Travellers are often motivated by racism and that those committed to getting Travellers out of the Borough will try to use the Criteria for this purpose. Therefore, the professional judgement of the Director of Environmental Health and Consumer Services will be crucial in determining whether the Criteria are met. Any decision to evict on nuisance grounds cannot go ahead until the Travellers on the site are made aware of what the Council expects from them, and eviction should only be adopted as a last resort, if the occupants of the site refuse to co-operate with the Council, and fail consistently to meet the demands of the nuisance criteria. When operating the criteria, the Council must take into account the fact that some Travellers' livelihoods depend on the clearance of builders' rubble and rubbish, and every effort must be made to advise and assist the Travellers to dispose of rubbish and rubble in the proper way.

These nuisance criteria were adopted at the Race and Community Relations Committee of 18 March 1987 despite concerns expressed by Camden Committee for Community Relations (CCCR) following consultation with Travellers. Their view was that a decision to evict Travellers for causing intentional damage "perhaps constitutes firmer action than that in respect of other groups of people" and that "evidence" of ward councillors should be considered rather than their "views" to ensure more objectivity in implementing the criteria (j).

Following those policy changes with respect to Travellers on sites, there were also changes in store for Travellers in homeless accommodation.

Overview: September 1987-December 1987

Between September 1987 and December 1987 Camden had moved from being recognised as a progressive local authority in terms of its service to homeless people, to a position where it ended up trying to defend in Court its failure to provide even the minimum service to homeless people in the Borough.

On 21 September Camden Labour Group agreed to tighten the criteria under which people would be considered as homeless in Camden. On 7 October Camden's Housing Management Executive Sub-Committee agreed that if the local authority of an individual presenting themselves to Camden could provide reasonable accommodation for him/her, the individual would be referred back to that authority regardless of which part of the world it was in. Although it is known that a number of Irish families, including Travellers, were given travel warrants to return to Ireland in accordance with Camden's new policy, exact statistics are not available.

On Friday 13 November Camden's policies towards the homeless made front page news in the *Guardian*, in an article which reported that as well as "repatriating" homeless Irish families "Camden were considering offering airline tickets to two Bangladeshi families who "had presented themselves as homeless in circumstances where, had they come from Ireland, decisions would be made which would avoid a call on Camden's housing resources" (*Guardian* 13 November, 1987).

On Monday 16 November Camden's Labour Group met, amid calls for the resignation of the Chair of the Housing Management Committee, Councillor Gareth Smyth, and voted to continue operating the so-called

---

(j)   Decisions, Race and Community Relations Committee 18.9.87.

"repatriation policy" but only with regard to Irish people! Travel warrants continued to be issued to homeless Irish families.

On 9 October when Camden HPS staff reported for work as usual they found Camden Security waiting at the door of Instrument House, where the Section was based, preventing entry. All staff were given a letter informing them that they were to be on two weeks "special leave" with full pay while an internal audit was conducted in HPS in response to allegations that Camden had paid £8m to house 650 non-existent families in B&B. Staff wishing to collect personal effects from the building were accompanied to their desks by individual security staff.

Later that day, at a meeting with the Director of Housing, it was made known to HPS staff that they were not guaranteed a job and that as from Monday 12 October the HPS would no longer be in existence as it had been. The letter given to staff intimated that, as yet, individuals in the Section were not deemed culpable for any discrepancy.

During these two weeks, HPS staff struggled to provide a service to homeless people. After several days of no service at all, a skeleton staff began to operate from Bidborough House, trying to provide a service without access to their HPS records and with only the resource of the telephone. Closing HPS while the audit was conducted not only left homeless people totally bereft, but also had a devastating effect on HPS staff, left to work in appalling conditions, with the anxiety of not knowing what was going to happen to their section.

On 10 November 1987, Camden Nalgo released the following statement in response to the closure of HPS and media coverage of the event, which they claimed had been used by leading Labour Councillors as an opportunity to criminalise and stigmatise the HPS staff, and "dub as scroungers" homeless people in Camden.

"The facts now revealed *by the Council's own investigation* show this media exercise to be a publicity fraud pursued for internal political reasons.

What is the truth?
1. The figures for 'ghost' families quoted above arising from a hotel check carried out in September 1987 cannot be substantiated. The Director of Housing on 9 October told staff that they had been calculated "on the back of an envelope". The more systematic calculation reveals a possible discrepancy of under 50 families.
2. The possible financial loss was grossly and dishonestly exaggerated at the outset. The Director of Finance reports that the probable loss is

in the region of, not *£8 million* but *£1.3 million*; and even this estimate is open to doubt. The loss arises largely from the policy, *carried out at the instructions of management*, of block booking hotels.

3. Councillors and the media have implied that staff may have been involved in fraud or 'a racket' and have therefore been suspended. In fact, staff in HPS have *at no time been suspended*. They were initially put on special paid leave for two weeks, later reduced to ten days. They have been providing a restricted emergency service to the homeless since 20 October and have been working normally from their office at Instrument House since 9 November. At no time has Councillor Smyth or any other Council representative sought to set the record straight by publicising *these* facts.

4. Councillor Dykes has claimed ignorance of any problems in the Unit prior to October 1987. In reality:

— In June 1986 a request was made for Income Recovery Officers for the Unit. They were not appointed until December 1986 and then with no proper line of management accountability. Once appointed these staff were instructed not to attempt to recover bed and breakfast payments from clients. These payments are now irretrievable and are still running at circa £2 million per annum.

— The post to check hotel invoices has been vacant and frozen for six months so that HPS is now totally reliant on the honesty of hoteliers when paying invoices.

— A backlog of cases was allowed to build up for 18 months despite repeated calls from staff for action. In April 1987 staff were *instructed* to 'rubber stamp' 1,500 applications with no checks being made or assessment of their claims.

— In March and May 1987 the HPS Shop passed *motions of no confidence* in its management's ability to tackle the section's problems. These were given to Councillor Dykes and the Housing Management Committee. To date no replies have been received.

— For at least two years staff have called for an investigation into HPU to deal with exactly those problems "revealed" by the current Audit.

— The true responsibility for the admitted inefficiency and lack of clear financial systems and policy guidelines which have afflicted the service is made clear by the interim report of the Director of Finance (Para.5.2):

'It is the responsibility of management to establish the necessary systems to protect the Council's interests and this has not been done, despite reports by both internal and external auditors dating back over several years'.

The final Audit report, far from finding dishonesty amongst staff, can only show a severe failure of senior managers and Councillors in the administration of the Homeless Persons Service".

It was alleged by the Manifesto Group of Labour Councillors[9] on 7 December 1987 that what they described as "the attack on the Homeless Persons Unit" had been:

"Not an accident or a management failure, but a politically determined policy to reduce expenditure by cutting a front line service to those most in need and with least power to fight".

In the light of the serious nature of the policy decisions made in Camden in September 1987, it is important to trace some of the events which made national news back to their source.

Policy changes

On 21 September 1987 Councillor Smyth Chair of the Housing Management Committee, addressing the Camden Labour Group on the issue of homelessness, told the meeting that they must adopt an emergency programme to get people out of bed and breakfast and tighten up areas where there was a statutory responsibility to house. This would not include using racist precedents such as in the Tower Hamlets case or sending battered women home but with that exception it was proposed to use The Bristol Case ex parte Browne. This case concerned a woman from the Republic of Ireland who was refused accommodation by Bristol City Council on the grounds that accommodation was available to her in Tralee, even though she was fleeing domestic violence there and Tralee was outside the jurisdiction of the Homeless Persons Act (see Appendix II). This option would give a sound basis for campaigning, give breathing space for discussions and would provide a format by which Camden could argue that it could not solve the homelessness crisis alone. In a written report to the Labour Group, Councillor Smyth pointed out that the Council faced a situation in which spending on bed and breakfast was currently £20.4 million, a figure which the Council could not afford.

"In this situation decisions will have to be reached, decisions which we will not find palatable".

He placed responsibility for the homelessness crisis at the door of the

Government who "have created misery and hardship through their ideological commitment to 'free market' economics".

His report recommended:

"1. That we tighten up on our acceptance as described in 4.3.1.

4.3.1. *Tightening up on who we accept*

Policies towards the homeless would be reviewed to ensure that Camden accepts no more households than the law requires, thus bringing Camden into line with other Labour Boroughs. This means not only a prompt assessment and decision making process with adequate staff to do this work to ensure speedy turn round of cases but also a rigorous interpretation of the legal position on reasonableness of accommodation, intentionality, local connection, and vulnerability. I will issue an instruction that we do not use the Tower Hamlets precedent.

Applicants dissatisfied with particular decisions can go to law to seek judicial review — all such actions would be defended.

2. That we adopt an emergency programme to get people out of bed and breakfast as described in 4.3.2.

4.3.2. *An Emergency programme to get people out of Bed and Breakfast*

A detailed check of hotels and HPS records is now underway to establish the actual position using temporarily seconded staff. A review is being carried out of all possible resources to get the homeless out of bed and breakfast, including:

1. Bringing back into use unmodernised hostels (54 bed spaces).
2. Checking accepted voids and issuing an ultimatum to take up occupation (33 units).
3. Checking voids under repair to see if occupancy can be taken up now and repairs done later.
4. Reviewing voids previously held for capital programme to see if they can be used now (figure not yet known).
5. Auditing Stage II and PSL properties to see if they are really occupied to bring back into use all those as fast as possible (112 units). Total 199 Units.
6. Reviewing potential rehousing resources to year end if all other rehousing ceased. These figures allow for 50 units to be reserved for emergency rehousing eg essential repairs transfers, medical As etc.

     349   1 beds

     284   2 beds +

Total 633

7. LAMS resources for next six month period are estimated at 66 units.
8. A one offer housing policy would produce a further 40 units. Total 938 Units.

The rate plan provided for 1,005 households in bed and breakfast. The current number is 1593.

At current rates of admission there will be 2207 households in bed and breakfast by the end of the year. If we adopt the measures outlined in 4.3.1 and 4.3.2 there will be 1186 households in bed and breakfast by the end of the year. It is estimated that this will save £2.3m of the £9.536 overspend.

3. That subject to consultation with staff we seek a management structure that will enable us to support and direct these initiatives.
4. That all Councillors and Officers support the strategy outlined and that we go on to a campaigning offensive forthwith to explain the reasons for homelessness and to demand, with public support, that the Government recognises the scale of the problem and takes appropriate action".

Councillor Smyth's proposals as amended by his speech and two other amendments that were carried, were voted on and passed by 25 votes to 15 with one abstention. Four amendments were lost when put to the vote. Significantly and of great consequence to Travellers one of these was:

"We will not adopt policies and practices which clearly have no basis in law, eg turning away applicants who are homeless and in priority need and who have no local connection with Camden or any other authority in Britain".

This was lost by 25 votes to 16.

Councillor Smyth claimed not to be following the racist precedent of Tower Hamlets Council in its wholesale eviction of Bengali families. However, whatever Camden's intentions were, most public criticism of this policy change drew a direct parallel with the Tower Hamlets action. The issue of Camden's own treatment of homeless Bengali families had previously hit the headlines in 1984. The death of a Bengali family in an hotel used by HPS caused an upsurge of anger in the black community culminating in the occupation of Camden Town Hall. it could be suggested in fact that the parallel lay closer to home.

Some effects of the policy changes

As part of this attempt by Camden to save money on the B&B bill, an intensive non-residency check was carried out in mid-September 1987 using temporarily seconded staff as well as HPS staff. This involved visiting the hotel rooms of all Camden's B&B clients, to establish if they were resident.

On 3 July 1987 procedures for HPS staff to follow in the matter of non-residency were drawn up, as follows:

"2.0 *Permitted away from hotels*
2.1 Households staying away from the hotel for one to three nights must inform the hotel management, who in turn should inform HPS.
2.2 Households wishing to stay out for more than three nights must seek permission in advance from HPS, and a note must be made in the non-residence book.
2.3 Hotel bookings will be kept open for two weeks for annual holiday, at the discretion of the Senior Housing Adviser. Permission should not be granted to households booked in for a short period pending investigation. Other absences in excess of three days may be approved by the Senior, e.g. to visit sick relatives, attend a funeral, etc.
2.4 Housing Advisers should tell households to inform DHSS about any absences. Failure to do so could lead to loss of benefit, and, consequently, accommodation.

3.0 *Non-residence without permission*
3.1 Households who stay away from the hotel without permission will have their booking cancelled *after discussion with the appropriate adviser team*. Re-booking is at the discretion of the Senior Adviser following discussion between the client and an adviser. It will only be agreed where there are extenuating circumstances. It will not usually be possible to re-book in the same hotel.
3.2 Where only some members of the household are resident the booking for the entire household will be cancelled.

4.0 *Reports and Investigations*
4.1 If an investigation by Council staff shows a household has been non-resident without permission, the booking will be cancelled, following the procedure laid out in 3.1.
4.2 If a hotel reports non-residence or if a DHSS or other third party report of non-residence is confirmed by the hotel, the booking will be cancelled. However, unless a follow-up investigation is

made by Council staff at the hotel, clients who approach the section with a reasonable explanation must be re-booked.

5.0 *Warnings*

5.1 When the Senior Adviser uses their discretion to re-book households who have been non-resident, a written warning should be issued to the household. A copy of the warning will be kept on the client's file, and it will be noted in the non-residence book that a warning has been issued. Having received a warning, a household will not be re-booked if there is a second firm report of non-residence."

Because of lack of resources Camden has tended not to carry out regular non-residency checks. The idea behind the checks is to ensure that only homeless families are placed in B&B. As a result of this particular check, one Traveller family who had been in B&B for almost two years, were made homeless. The family had been out during the day of 24 September and had come back to find a letter waiting for them at reception, saying that their B&B had been cancelled. They were shocked but could not get hold of anyone to whom they could put their case, so they left the hotel to find relatives to stay with overnight. The next day they went to Camden Community Law Centre. According to the family, they had been staying in the hotel and had signed the register. Not only that, but they had left clothes in their rooms in the hotel, and other items such as cups and plates, as well as a baby's buggy. When the law centre contacted Camden HPS about the check, they were told that a proper decision had been made by staff, who had the support of management. The HPS were prepared to defend the decision in Court if necessary.

As well as the procedures already outlined regarding non-residency, there was a checklist given to those staff who carried out the non-residency check which read as follows:

"CHECKLIST TO ESTABLISH RESIDENCY/NON RESIDENCY
Personal possessions, clothing in wardrobes/drawers, letters, newspapers — check dates — cooking utensils, stored food in room/fridge — fresh or rotten — have beds been slept in — when was linen changed, towels used, wash basins, presence of soap, toothpaste, toothbrush etc.

COMMENTS FROM HOTEL STAFF: When last seen in hotel, have

they signed register, are all household members always present or only some etc."

The Law Centre contacted Camden's Central Race Relations Unit about the family, who then came to the Unit. The researcher was the only person available that day who worked with Travellers. Because of the urgency of the situation, the researcher spoke to the HPS manager on the family's behalf. The response was that it was the word of HPS staff against the word of the family, and in such circumstances the manager would support the staff's decision. The only way such a decision could be challenged was through the Courts. Pointing out that the family had nowhere to go in the meantime only elicited a shrug.

The researcher then telephoned the manager of the hotel the family had been in, who said that the family's B&B had not in fact been cancelled by Camden. Unless it was cancelled that afternoon, then the family's rooms would be paid for over the weekend which meant they would not be on the streets, but could go back to the hotel.

The manager agreed, on request, to go to the family's rooms and check if there were any belongings in them. The researcher waited on the telephone while he did this. He came back to the telephone and gave exactly the account the family had given of what was in the rooms. He also confirmed that on the day he gave the family the letter they left immediately without going to their rooms. The law centre was made aware of this. The hotel manager also commented that he was fed up with the Council because the belongings of another family whose B&B had been cancelled that day as a result of the non-residency check, were cluttering up the corridor!

By the following Tuesday the family's B&B was cancelled by Camden and they had nowhere to go. Attempts to get social services to take an interest failed dismally. The researcher was told they were only dealing with "life and limb" emergencies. Even the Director of Social Services could do nothing. The Camden out of hours Social Services workers would not touch any case related to HPS. The Travellers Outreach Worker contacted, as a last resort the Chair of the Race Committee in an attempt to find accommodation for the family who by now were exhausted, bewildered, angry and desperate. This resulted in a conversation with the Assistant Director of Housing (Needs) who merely said that should the family in question care to seek a judicial review they were free to do so, but the decision about their non-residency status had been made and he was concerned about his staff's morale.

Several other Traveller families were made homeless as a result of this non-residency check, which would appear not to have been carried out according to the criteria on the checklist used by staff.

The last contact of the researcher with this family was when they left to go again to the Law Centre, who had agreed to take their case.

This family became homeless again after almost two years of B&B life waiting to be rehoused, on the word of a council officer who apparently could only be made accountable in a court of law.

Bureaucracies can make mistakes — but here there was no appeals procedure for the family to utilise nor was there any chance of their circumstances being further investigated.

Non-residency

This issue of non-residency is a vexed one. HPS staff claim that many Travellers, having been booked into an hotel, only stay a short time and then move away, only to return again months later and reapproach as homeless. It has been put forward that the reason for this is that Travellers are not homeless at all to begin with, but rather need an address from which to claim welfare benefits. In this way it is concluded that a number of Travellers approaching Camden HPS do not have a housing problem but do have a problem in claiming benefits. In September 1986, in a report on the Travellers policy in the Borough, the Chair of the Race Committee had this to say about Travellers and welfare benefits:

> "The Welfare Rights Adviser reports that problems facing Travellers claiming Supplementary Benefit in Camden have centred mainly around verification of identity both for themselves and their children. Basically, the DHSS will not accept that Travellers are who they say they are unless they can prove 'their identity'."

One local DHSS office makes no secret of their view that all Travellers claims should be treated with the utmost suspicion, having told the council that "90 per cent of all Travellers claims are fraudulent". When asked how they knew this, the answer had seemed to be, "because if we did not pay them they go away". The fact that some Travellers live in B&B accommodation (homeless, hotel dwellers being another target for heavy fraud investigations) has done nothing to dispel the strongly held prejudices of some DHSS officers. The DHSS is supported in their view by the instructions in circular S50/85 entitled "Verification of Identity — Preventing Fraud" (see Appendix III). One of the most vexing problems

56

for Travellers is the provision of documentary evidence of identity when their lifestyles often militate against the preservation of original documents like birth certificates. The "S50" circular advises "recently issued copy certificates" should not be acceptable on their own, and that baptism certificates are "easily obtained and forged". One area social services officer in Camden was finding that duty social workers were overwhelmed with requests for financial help from homeless families, particularly Irish Travellers, who had been refused supplementary benefit altogether.

The tactics of fighting this blanket approach by the DHSS were carefully considered. Legal opinion was sought on the possibility of going through a judicial review — since it seemed that Travellers as a group were being discriminated against. In the event Camden was advised by Counsel to try local appeals against the refusal of welfare benefits. The first appeal was successful and demonstrated a way around challenging the Secretary of State's decisions and exploiting the DHSS' lack of preparation of evidence to prove fraud. The Tribunal found that the claimant was "entitled to supplementary benefit for himself and his family — since there was no conclusive proof of fraud, and that, in their view, there was no reason not to accept the documentary evidence provided by the families".

Another problem Travellers face is trying to prove they live on sites. The DHSS insist on visiting caravans before they will accept them as a permanent address. This can take up to six weeks, during which time the Travellers have no money. This difficulty is compounded by the possibility of the family being evicted before they can be visited, which means that a whole cycle can develop of making a claim, waiting for a visit, being evicted, finding somewhere else to stay, making yet another claim and all the time having to survive without any help from the DHSS.

The problem is directly related to the lack of official site provision in Camden. If official sites existed, then an official address would be available, which would undoubtedly ease the situation for Travellers.

Travellers interviewed in the course of this research, were often experiencing problems with claiming benefits. One man remarked that he "did not expect such hassle after settling down".

Another woman waited for three months to get her payments, and another family are at the time of writing still waiting for Child Benefit to come through since August 1987.

In terms of the claim that Travellers go into B&B simply to claim benefit, it is the experience of the Travellers' Outreach Worker that it is extremely difficult for Travellers to get their benefit entitlement regardless of where they are because of problems with suspicion of fraud on grounds of being both Irish and Travellers. She cited a case where one Travelling woman had to live on Section One money[10] for 10 months because of difficulties in claiming from the DHSS, and said that even after winning the appeal, it is still proving very difficult to extract benefit from the DHSS.

In the light of this it would appear that non-residence in the case of Travellers is not simply linked to difficulties with obtaining welfare benefits without having a permanent address. That is not to say that for some Travellers, this is not a factor.

Non-residence is linked to the conditions that cause Travellers to present as homeless in the first place, as already described in this report. As we have seen, hardship linked to lack of site provision, and harassment by the police; problems caused by illness and material poverty, and the difficulty of obtaining an education for their children mean that some families feel unable any longer to sustain the travelling way of life and they approach as homeless and are booked into a hotel. Before long they find that hotel life is not any real alternative to travelling as far as they are concerned, because although the difficulties involved are different, they are often increased by being isolated from other Travellers and losing the support network of the Travelling Community. Finding themselves cooped up in a hotel with small children, and having to adapt to a whole new lifestyle is a tremendously difficult experience. The hostility experienced from other residents, and aggressive behaviour from hoteliers, along with all the stress encountered by homeless people living in hotels, may prove to be such that a Traveller family decide that life on the road is preferable, after all. However, while one set of circumstances may appear more manageable than another, in reality, Travellers fall between two alternatives, neither of which hold out much hope of stability. I would suggest that this situation could offer an explanation for the phenomenon described by HPS staff of being booked into a hotel and before long, leaving it, only to return at some later stage.

The important thing here is to recognise that this does not in any way detract from the genuine status of the family as homeless. A service such as that provided by Camden HPS relies to an extent on acceptance of an individual or household's claim, backed by evidence, that they are indeed homeless and in priority need. It is of course, possible to be homeless more than once, and in the case of Travellers[10] who are operating under so many restrictions to their way of life, this is a likely scenario.

At the root of this lies the lack of responsibility demonstrated not only by Camden but by many other local authorities, in refusing to make provision for Travelling people in their locality a serious priority. It is shameful that a minority group should be enduring such constant disregard that their very existence as a distinct community is under threat.

Travel warrants: a policy of "repatriation"

The policy change which has had most impact on Travellers has been that which has resulted in an unknown number of Irish families being given travel warrants to return to Ireland on grounds that they had no local connection with Camden and that they had either made themselves intentionally homeless by leaving a tenancy they could "reasonably occupy" in Ireland, or that they were unintentionally homeless but that the local authority in Ireland from whence they had come had undertaken to offer them "suitable" accommodation.

According to Section 67 of the Housing Act 1985 (part iii):

"(1) If the local housing authority —

    a) are satisfied that an applicant is homeless and has a priority need, and are not satisfied that he became homeless intentionally, but

    b) are of opinion that the conditions are satisfied for referral of his application to another local housing authority in England, Wales or Scotland, they may notify that other authority of the fact that his application has been made and that they are of that opinion.

(2) The conditions for referral of an application to another local housing authority are —

    a) that neither the applicant nor any person who might reasonably be expected to reside with him has a local connection with the district of the authority to whom his application was made.

    b) that the applicant or a person who might reasonably be expected to reside with him has a local connection with the district of that other authority, and

    c) that neither the applicant nor any person who might reasonably be expected to reside with him will run the risk of domestic violence in that other district".

Under Section 66 of the Act, where an authority are satisfied that an applicant has priority need but are also satisfied that he became threatened with homeless intentionally, "they shall furnish him with advice and such assistance as they consider appropriate in the circumstances in any attempts he may make to secure that accommodation does not cease to be available for his occupation" (66 (3) (c)).

The Housing Act 1985 (part iii), and the Homeless Persons Act (1977) both refer specifically to England, Scotland and Wales. This does not include any part of Ireland.

Camden's decision in September 1987 to use the precedent set by R. v. Bristol ex parte Browne, (see Appendix II) means that it is now Camden's policy to refer priority need homeless people who come to Camden from outside England, Scotland, and Wales (and who have no local connection with the Borough) back to the local authority from whence they came, if and only if that local authority is prepared to offer them suitable accommodation.

In a draft policy statement on homelessness which is being used as working practice in the HPS, the Council's policy is laid out as follows.

"A2 — Homelessness
In circumstances where a person presents as homeless having come from outside England, Wales, or Scotland, the council recognises that the person is homeless, but will consider whether that person is intentionally homeless. (See paragraph 6 below).

6. Intentional Homelessness
The Council will consider the circumstances of all those presenting as homeless from the point of view of intentional homelessness, if it appears that the applicant has deliberately done something, or failed to do something which has had the consequence that s/he has ceased to occupy available accommodation which it would have been reasonable for him/her to continue to occupy.

The Council will take all relevant factors into account in individual cases, and, if the facts require it, will make a decision of intentional homelessness.

There is a variety of circumstances which could lead to a decision of intentional homelessness, including rent arrears, failure to pay mortgage payments, failure to defend possession proceedings, causing nuisance or annoyance to neighbours resulting in eviction, leaving settled accommodation to move into unsettled accommodation, loss of tied accommodation and so on.

The Council will look back into the applicant's history of residence as far as is necessary to identify circumstances, if any, in which an applicant left settled accommodation which was suitable for his/her occupation. "Suitable Accommodation" will be considered in relation to the housing situation prevailing in the area of the London Borough of Camden.

Enquiries into these circumstances will be made in respect of persons presenting as homeless to the Council having left accommodation in places outside England, Scotland and Wales, applying the same considerations as those affecting applicants from England, Scotland and Wales".

The policy has proved extremely controversial, with Camden being accused of operating an immigration control via the Housing Department, and a policy of "repatriation". Since the implementation of the policy the debate has continued to rage and the Council have continued to defend the policy.

In answer to remarks by Ken Livingstone, MP, criticising Camden's policy in terms of its effects on homeless Irish people, Councillor Smyth said:

> *"We have 11,000 people on our waiting list and around 4,000 people in Bed and Breakfast. We have had no block grant since 1980 and have been rate capped since 1986. In these circumstances the majority group in Camden decided it was not unreasonable to treat Irish people with no local connection with the Borough as we would treat those coming from Pontypridd, Liverpool, or Edinburgh".* (Ham and High *November 27th 1987*).

What seems to have escaped Councillor Smyth is the fact that the 26 county state in Ireland is not part of the United Kingdom, it is an independent state with its own laws. To claim that Irish people receive the same treatment as those from Pontypridd and Liverpool is false, because a local authority in England, Scotland or Wales has a legal duty to accommodate anyone who has been referred back to them from another local authority, while the same legislation does not exist in the Irish 26 county state. What this means is that there is no real guarantee that people referred back will be given accommodation on their return.

HPS staff have said they were told to apply the policy to all homeless Irish families, including those already being housed temporarily by the Council.

Despite Camden's assurances that they would send people with no local connection back to the local authority from whence they came if and only if that local authority was prepared to offer them suitable accommodation several families were offered travel warrants where the only assurance from the Irish authority was that the family could claim the equivalent of housing benefit if they managed to obtain their own accommodation.

According to the Travellers Rights Organisation several Traveller families' offer of suitable accommodation was the same flat in Dublin's Ballymin, and it was in such a state of disrepair that it was uninhabitable. As each family refused to take the flat, it was re-offered to Camden for the next Traveller family being given a travel warrant.

Trying to monitor the number of travel warrants that have been issued by Camden to Traveller families is difficult. There is no record in HPS of how many have been given. Going through the "discharged 1987" box in HPS, there were eight cards belonging to Traveller families which clearly stated that a travel warrant had been issued.

One of these warrants was issued in January 1987 and one in June 1987. Two were issued in September 1987 and four were issued in October 1987.

It was recorded on the cards of two of the families that they had refused the travel warrants. One of the eight families was given a warrant after having spent several months placed in a B&B hotel by Camden. Five of the families were given warrants on the same day they approached the HPS as homeless. One more Traveller family was given a warrant in February 1988 also on the same day of approaching as homeless. Unfortunately for Camden, because of the ferry strike, they were obliged to accommodate the family until such time as they could travel back to Ireland.

From October 1987-February 1988 decisions on all HPS cases were being made by the Assistant Director of Housing (Needs). If an applicant managed to get through on the telephone to HPS they would be booked into an hotel for one night and told to telephone the HPS in the morning, for a decision on their case.

It was not until the end of November 1987 that staff were given the draft policy statement on homelessness to work from, and in between times, much confusion surrounded decisions being made in the HPS.

Difficulty with getting through on the telephone to HPS meant that some applicants booked in for one night stayed on in hotels for weeks, especially in the block-booked hotels. These were new referrals which could not be dealt with.

In an effort to pacify community and voluntary groups who were enraged at the policy changes and the continued closure of the HPS, the Assistant Director of Housing (Needs) did agree to see some homeless people and did take some telephone calls in the afternoons at the Housing Department.

Despite this, many homeless people complained of having been turned away from the Housing Department without seeing anybody or receiving any help. Complaints were made that the Assistant Director of Housing (Needs) "hung up" the telephone on homeless families, some of whom eventually make their way to his office to protest at the treatment they were receiving.

A high court action is being taken by SHAC — the London Housing Aid Centre — on behalf of various voluntary groups in Camden, which is challenging the Council's policy of offering travel warrants to homeless Irish people instead of housing them. Camden Community Law Centre has already successfully challenged four cases where families were offered warrants or were asked at short notice to vacate council-funded accommodation.

On 20 November 1987, after the Council's policy had made front-page news in the *Guardian*, Camden asked the Association of London Authorities to review the policies, procedure and strategy followed by the Council when families apply as homeless and to make recommendations in the light of what other London Boroughs do.

Despite all the publicity that has surrounded this policy, one thing that has not been given much space is the fact that this is not the first attempt made by Camden to introduce such a policy.

On 10 March 1987, as part of the housing budget review report submitted by Policy and Resources Committee, proposals were put forward concerning such referral rights back to Ireland. These were submitted under the heading "Travellers".

The report claimed that Travellers constituted 17 per cent of the people in bed and breakfast and alleged that they accounted for 30 per cent of the net bed and breakfast bill. As a response to these figures it was recommended that the new Government in the 26 county Irish state should be lobbied on two counts:

1. *"To introduce homelessness legislation including referral rights back to Ireland (Eire) from the UK of people with known addresses.*
2. *To enter into joint funding arrangements for sites in the UK for people from Eire with no address to be referred back to".*

In these proposals, from the Director of Housing, Travellers were being isolated as a group who should be denied a council service, so that the

63

Council could find ways of reducing expenditure on the bed and breakfast bill.

It is significant that here again the jump-off point is statistics from the Housing Department as to the number of Travellers in B&B. It would appear to be the view of the Director of Housing that the Irish 26 county state government has a responsibility to look after those of its nationals who emigrate, even to providing accommodation for them in another country! Clearly there is a limit in the mind of senior management in the Housing Department as to the number of homeless Travellers to be permitted.

In response to these proposals a number of organisations expressed concern that such a policy, if endorsed, could be racially discriminatory, and could contravene other rights of Irish people as EEC citizens, as well as contravening the Race Relations Act (1976).

It was pointed out that referral rights back to Ireland would be a direct contravention of existing legislation such as the Homeless Persons Act 1977 and the Housing Act (part iii) 1985, which refer specifically to England, Scotland and Wales. It would also contravene the rights of Irish people to come freely to Britain under the common travel area agreement, and the Government of Ireland Act 1949, as well as their freedom of movement as EEC citizens. Camden's own Race and Community Relations Committee made strong objections to the proposals, on the grounds already mentioned, and also expressed concern that the proposals had not been cleared with regard to legal implications before submission to Committee. Once these proposals were approved, they could logically be directed at any other ethnic grouping placing demand on the Council for housing. To implement the proposals would require a degree of immigration control within the HPS and present the risk that the police might be drawn into the HPS in terms of implementation of immigration legislation.

The Travellers Officer Group, comprising representatives from different Council departments concerned with implementing the non-harassment policy, as well as representatives from outside agencies, made strong objections to the proposals in principle because they advocated discrimination on grounds of race, nationality or ethnic origin. The group noted that policies and practices with regard to Travellers had become less sympathetic to the needs of Travellers over the year, and that more recognition was now being given to the views of those prejudiced against Travellers. It also found it to be unacceptable that when financial resources become inadequate to meet total demand for services, the Council should seek to discredit the needs of immigrants to the country and turn them away so that resources can be concentrated on those already resident in Great Britain.

When the Assistant Director of Housing (Needs) was challenged about the proposals at the Travellers Officers Group on 23 April 1987, he replied that under part iii of the Housing Act (1985), anyone presenting as homeless with an address elsewhere in the UK (with the exception of Northern Ireland) could be referred back to the local authority from whence they came. If they were homeless but had an obvious local connection elsewhere within the UK they could also be referred back. It was because of the anomaly regarding Irish nationals that the proposals had been put forward.

There are a number of problems with such an argument. Firstly, to describe the position of Irish Nationals as an anomaly is an absurdity. Their position is identical to that of any other foreign national who makes an application as a homeless person in England, Scotland or Wales. Secondly, this argument makes a distinction between Irish Nationals and people from Northern Ireland. In terms of British legislation on homelessness in fact, their positions are identical. The Assistant Director was trying to imply that, far from being racist in singling out the Irish for special treatment, the Housing Department was attempting to apply equal treatment for everybody — everyone could be referred back to the area from which they came regardless of jurisdiction or the autonomy of another country. Such a fudging of the issues is only possible because of the confusion that exists in people's minds about the relationship between Britain and Ireland. Why did the proposal not include lobbying to extend homelessness legislation to Northern Ireland? (This is a call which has been made by housing organisations in Northern Ireland in terms of civil rights which they argue should extend to Northern Ireland if it is a normal part of the UK.)

The Assistant Director referred to the amount of money being spent on B&B accommodation for Travellers' families, and the Council's financial crisis. The line of argument he is using here suggests a purely pragmatic decision — Travellers from the Irish Republic seemed to be coming to Camden in unacceptable numbers, therefore some legalistic form had to be found to exclude them. He appeared to find it acceptable that Travellers should be isolated as a group in terms of how much they cost the Council.

This would appear to suggest that the March proposals were mounted specifically with Travellers in mind. The most vulnerable and abused

65

section of the Irish Community in Britain were the first targets for such discriminatory policies.

By September 1987 Camden had decided upon the so-called "repatriation" policy, and immediately implemented it.

The non-harassment policy in practice

Meanwhile the policy concerning Travellers on sites had not been faring well either.

In the four years since the Council first adopted the non-harassment policy, no permanent sites have been provided for Travellers in Camden. A grant application has been made to the Department of the Environment for the purchase and development of an existing unofficial site on Britannia Street, London WC1, as a permanent site for Travellers. Even if the Department of the Environment respond positively, the development of Britannia Street would be only a small contribution to permanent site provision in the Borough, as it could only provide 2-4 pitches for caravans. Given that there were recently up to 13 unofficial sites in Camden, this falls far short of meeting the need for sites in the Borough.

There is only one post in the Council which exists to defend the rights of Travellers. In addition, in the Council's present financial crisis, a cut of 16 per cent has been made to the budget allowed for the operating of the non-harassment policy.

The budget for the policy pays for the facilities on the unofficial sites in the Borough which makes it a frontline Council Service. A cut of 16 per cent means that the policy has to be amended to accommodate the cut, because the new budget will not meet the cost of the facilities needed. The 1987/88 budget will already be overspent, which indicates that need outstrips the provision being made even before a 16 per cent is administered. On 23 February 1988 a meeting was held about the Travellers policy, attended by five Councillors, including the Chairs of Policy and Resources, Councillor Satnam Gill; Housing, Councillor Gareth Smyth; Race, Councillor Barbara Beck; the Local Ward Councillor, Councillor Bill Saunders, and the Leader of the Council, Councillor Tony Dykes. Also present was the Travellers Outreach Worker and officers from other departments involved with the running of the non-harassment policy. In a report to the meeting, the Chair of Race had made five recommendations regarding the non-harassment policy:

1. That officers be instructed to progress the planning application to

develop Britannia Street as a permanent site as a matter of urgency.

2. That a permanent site for Travellers be included in the planning brief for the Kings Cross development, as proposed at the consultative meetings.

3. That a personal planning permission be granted on 94-96 Castlehaven Road to regularise the position of a Traveller family on the site, and that it be removed from the disposals list.

4. That officers be instructed to review the disposals list to identify any potential sites suitable for Travellers.

5. That the non-harassment policy be maintained in its present form and the necessary funds be found for 1988/89.

The first recommendation ran into trouble because the Leader of the Council made it clear that as far as the Labour Group were concerned, the present situation, where a grant application had been made for the purchase and development of a 2-4 pitch site on Britannia Street, was a subversion of Council policy, he maintained that it had never been agreed to develop a 4 pitch site, but only a 2 pitch site, which would be subject to planning permission anyway. The question which has to be asked here is, why was this situation not made clear before, given that the Chair of Race had been aware of all the developments on this?

Councillors also argued that Camden cannot realistically pursue the Travellers policy in isolation from neighbouring Boroughs because as long as they continue to swiftly evict Travellers then Camden will be taking on more than its fair share of responsibility for Travellers in the area. Nothing could proceed on Britannia Street until Members had seen all the correspondence connected with the site, and then decisions would be made.

The second recommendation was not viewed favourably. The decision as to whether a permanent site for Travellers be included in the planning brief for the Kings Cross development, is a decision for the Labour Group. The Leader pointed out that using land for a Travellers site would mean taking it away from other sectors of the community, and even if there were a site, it could not be expected that money would come from the Council to run the site, because of the financial crisis. In a written report to the meeting, the Chair of Race had drawn attention to the fact that at two out of five of the consultation meetings recently held on the development, members of the community had suggested that a small part of the huge development be used for a Travellers site. This was the only proposal from the consultation which has not yet been included in the brief for the whole site. A site would generate an amount of revenue from rent etc which would contribute to costs. It was pointed out then by the Leader of the Council that this meeting could not put a Travellers site in the planning brief but that it must come from a Planning Labour Group Meeting.

The reply to the third recommendation was "the land had been sold". Despite pleas on behalf of this family by the Chair of Race, only two options were put forward:

1. That the family be taken on for rehousing by the Housing Association who have bought the land.
2. That they be accepted by the Council's Housing Department on prima facie evidence.

The family have been living in Camden on Council land for seven years. They are supported by the local community, and have never been a source of difficulty for the Council. Their needs or their welfare were at no point being taken into consideration by the Council. When it was agreed at the meeting to negotiate the possibility of the family being taken on by the Housing Association, one of the Members made this comment:

"We should be seen to act as humane as we keep pretending we are".

It was brought to the attention of this project the following day that the land had not yet in fact been sold.[11]

Recommendation number four was immediately thrown out, on the grounds that in the present financial situation Members were not prepared to consider Travellers needs if it meant loss of income from disposal of land.

Recommendation number five introduced a discussion about the cost of running the non-harassment policy. Some Members attempted to link the cost of the non-harassment policy to the cost of clearing sites in the Borough after an occupation, the inference being that if there was no non-harassment policy then there would be no site clearance needed. In this context it was suggested that the cheapest thing the Council could do would be to discontinue the policy and it was pointed out that it might be necessary to do this in order to maintain budgets. At this point, the Travellers Outreach Worker made it clear that the Council could not run the non-harassment policy on the budget proposed of £46,000, but could only offer limited facilities, and in this situation decisions about how to share out the facilities available would have to be made.

Children on unofficial temporary site at Brittania Street.

The idea that the non harassment policy "encourages" Travellers into Camden is spurious. Travellers were in the borough long before the policy was adopted and will remain, regardless of the policies of the Council.

The most striking thing about this meeting was that not once were the needs of Travellers or their welfare taken into account. It was crystal clear that the members were essentially concerned, not about the dire effect of their decisions on the lives of Travellers in the Borough, but about the financial crisis of the Council, and the needs of house-dwellers and people working in the Borough near the proposed Travellers site — in that order. Travellers needs were continually measured against the needs of the house-dwellers, for playgrounds or open space and housing, and found wanting. The fact that Travellers in Camden have no security or hope of progress, was not taken into account.

Also, recent months have seen a spate of evictions in the Borough, and on one occasion possession was sought for a site without the Travellers Outreach Worker even being informed. This makes a charade of that part of the policy which states that no eviction may occur without a report first being made on the conditions likely to be faced by Travellers, if evicted.

As Camden's financial crisis deepens the possibility of site provision recedes rapidly and a serious question mark hangs over the future of the non-harassment policy. In the light of Camden's determination to make drastic cuts to nurseries and other front-line services, it seems realistic to expect that the Travellers budget may well become, like the Housing Department's Racial Harassment budget a luxury that the Council can no longer afford.

Thus, four years after the non-harassment policy was first adopted it is apparent that it has effectively been abandoned. Moreover, the two parts of the council's Travellers policy, concerning firstly those on sites and secondly those declaring themselves homeless, closely interact. Travellers are forced into homeless accommodation by the lack of site provision and other factors including harassment by landlords, police, residents and now the council. When attempting to avail themselves of their rights under homelessness legislation Travellers face discrimination within the general lack of adequate provision. It can be seen that the overall result is a squeezing out of Travellers from Camden.

Having started with an apparently radical policy towards Travellers, Camden ends up with a set of policies which result in this council carrying out a set of policies whose results are no different from Tory immigration policy. Camden has not just squeezed Travellers beyond its own boundaries but has pushed them out of Britain altogether. The parallels with Tower Hamlets Council's treatment of Bengalis are obvious.

Political will

How can the difference be explained between what the council did and what it said it would do?

The council's principal defence is the financial crisis caused by ever more central government spending restraints. Clearly, this is an important factor. Services for Travellers or other ethnic minority groups are by no means the only casualties of the financial crisis.

However, this research calls into question the claim that financial facts were the only ones in play.

Firstly the statement of intent which the non-harassment policy represented was not backed up by any coherent practical policy. Indeed the Travellers Outreach Worker (TOW) was not appointed until July 1985 — more than one year after the adoption of the policy. Previous to the TOW's appointment the only concrete reality the policy had was the Travellers Officers Group, an ad hoc collection of officers and other interested parties which, while raising Travellers' issues, was not responsible for practically implementing the policy. So at that point the situation was that Travellers were merely allowed to stay in places around the borough but no facilities or support were provided.

Secondly the overt use of the press by some local politicians can only have heightened already existing local antagonism towards Travellers, rather than decreasing it.

What the research shows is not only the lack of any coherent reality to the non-harassment policy, but it also points to another huge area, namely homelessness, where policy collapsed altogether.

The collapse of these two policies resulted in chaos. As has clearly been shown the Travellers in their day to day life were faced with confusion and uncertainty, which provided fertile ground for arbitrary decision making and discrimination.

The non-harassment policy was clearly under attack from its beginnings. However, the defence of the policy was anything but robust, and most importantly, its defenders found no way past the resistance vis a vis permanent sites. Residents at an early open meeting[12] had called for this action as the real change necessary but the council's choice was to ignore these residents. In fact there appears to have been no serious attempt to publicly engage in the political argument, for decent provision for Travellers.

This does seriously question the commitment of the council at any time to the policy and does open it to the charge of political posturing on equal opportunities at a time when this issue was less unpopular than at present. With the election of new councillors in May 1986 following electioneering which was likely to appeal to racist views, as outlined earlier, the demise of the policy only quickened its pace.

Another example of the way the non-harassment policy has become less and less of a priority for the Council is the way the Race and Community

Relations Committee were unable, over the course of two meetings, to discuss the Council's so-called "repatriation" policy. As a result of pressure from Camden's Black and Ethnic Minority Communities, a Special Emergency Race Committee on Homelessness was convened. However, when the agenda for the meeting appeared, it failed to address the key issue of "Repatriation", much less address it in terms of how it affects Travellers. A report on Travellers and Homelessness, was rejected by the Chair, who refused to even allow the item of Travellers and Homelessness to be on the Agenda. It was only after uproar that the issue was finally discussed, and even then it was a most unsatisfactory discussion, with most of the crucial questions left hanging in the air.

Furthermore, and most significantly, the "repatriation policy" — the most extreme example of the disintegration of any pro-Travellers policy, was first noted in March 1987, before the Tory general election success

and before the collapse of the council's financial tactics. Although there was again uproar at the Race and Community Relations Committee when it appeared then, only a very few months later it was acceptable policy for Camden. It was also first aimed specifically at Irish Travellers. The implication here being clearly that an equal opportunities approach to Travellers was politically expendable *before* the onset of the financial crisis.

The change in a nutshell

Following Camden's decision to adopt the "repatriation" policy, an article appeared in the *Daily Mail* entitled "Council 'must close door on homeless Irish tinkers'." According to this report: "The Irish, including thousands of tinkers travelling in caravans, have cost Camden Council £11 million in B&B hotels this year alone, said the Council's Labour Leader, Mr Tony Dykes".

It is interesting to compare this with Councillor Barbara Beck's reply to an article in the *Hampstead and Highgate Express* in August 1986, entitled "Travellers move into B&B and Camden picks up the Tab".

The article quoted "Labour sources" who "revealed that high numbers of Travellers were using B&B as an address in order to claim benefits, and that "eight per cent of homeless households had become so because of loss of caravan".

Councillor Beck replied:

"In Camden homeless people are given the treatment which the law requires. This includes Travellers. More and more people are giving up the Travelling way of life under the pressure of constant evictions and harassment. When they present themselves as homeless to other Councils they may well be refused because they have 'no local connection'. This neatly avoids their responsibility as the agency which has made them homeless in the first place.

Camden Council sticks by its legal obligations when it is clear that people — and Travellers are people too — have no connection anywhere else and rehouses them or places them in B&B.

This is a question of a legal obligation on the Council. So please do not make Travellers scapegoats for a situation which is not of their own making".

It is sobering to consider that Councillor Beck wrote this letter just 15 months before Camden began implementing and defending a policy of issuing travel warrants to homeless Irish families with no local connections.

6. Conclusion

This project set out to discover if Travellers are suffering discrimination in their contact with Camden HPS and in their experience of living in temporary accommodation, and to record the experience of Travellers approaching as homeless in Camden.

Of the 40 Traveller families we contacted, all wanted to be permanently housed, although three families said if they got a place on an official caravan site they would prefer it.

It seems clear that Travellers have been suffering discrimination in their experience of living in B&B, and that Camden Council have discriminated against Travellers by implementing neither their Council-wide non-harassment policy, nor the HPS policy of withdrawing from any hotel refusing to place a homeless family. The procedures adopted by the HPS with regard to non-residency and moves between hotels are also open to being used in a discriminatory way towards Travellers.

The Council's repatriation policy, which was decided upon without any consultation with the Council's own Central Race Relations Unit, is directly discriminatory towards Travellers approaching as homeless in the Borough. Camden's failure to provide any permanent site for Travellers in the Borough, which has contributed directly to the situation homeless Travellers find themselves in, and the 16 per cent cut to the budget for running the non-harassment policy for 1988/99 indicates a lack of political commitment to meeting the needs of Travelling people in Camden.

With the increased use of the Public Order Act against Travellers it is now more urgent than ever that local Councils like Camden who have adopted a progressive policy towards Travellers, do not back-pedal on their commitment because of difficulties experienced as a result of financial constraints. Camden have complained bitterly that because they have operated in a non-discriminatory way towards Travellers, they have had to "pick up the tab" for other local Councils who evict Travellers speedily from their land and offer them travel warrants instead of housing. It is imperative that Camden do not measure their service to Travellers against the lack of provision made by other local authorities. The yardstick for assessing the adequacy of Camden's policies and practices must be whether or not the Traveller's needs are being met in the Borough.

The point of view of the Travelling Community must be given a hearing in the Council and must be taken into account when policy decisions are being made. Otherwise Travellers will continue to suffer discrimination in their dealings with the Council, both in terms of lack of site provision and their contact with the Housing Department.

7. Recommendations

In the light of the issues raised in this report it is recommended:

1. That Camden Council immediately discontinue the policy of offering travel warrants to homeless Irish families with no local connection with the Borough.

2. That Camden ensure the implementation of the Council-wide non-harassment policy of Travellers using any Council service.

3. That the need for permanent sites for Travellers be taken seriously as a matter of urgency, and that appropriate action be taken.

4. That maintaining the non-harassment policy be made a priority and that the Council recognise and acknowledge that the budget is inadequate, in terms of the need for facilities on unofficial sites in the Borough.

5. To develop policy in HPS, in conjunction with the Central Race Relations Unit and Travellers Officers Group, to take account of the particular needs of Travellers presenting as homeless.[13]

6. That Camden's policy of withdrawing from hotels refusing any homeless family be rigorously implemented.

7. That the Council review its present procedures concerning moves between hotels and non-residency in the light of their potentially discriminatory nature, particularly with regard to Travellers, and ensure that homeless families have an appeals procedure to resort to when their B&B is cancelled as a result of a non-residency check.

8. To increase the number of Hotels Officers and Environmental Health Officers to ensure adequate monitoring of hotels' practice and conditions.

9. Increase the staff of the Homeless Families playteam to ensure their valuable work reaches more families.

10. To consider, in conjunction with the Central Race Relations Unit and the Travellers Officer Group, what other resources the Council should make available to Travellers to ensure they are not discriminated against.

Notes

1. Minceir Misli: 90 Meath Street, Dublin 8 — "founded in 1984 among roadside Travellers Minceir Misli is a movement actively involved in the campaign against poverty, social exclusion, as well as a forum for thought and discussion among the Travelling people themselves and the wider society" — Minceir Misli founding leaflet 1984.

2. For an account of the struggles of Travellers and the conditions they experience at the hands of Dublin County Council see "Biting the Bullet — Authority and the Travellers" *Magill* Magazine April 1984.

3. In the period 1760-1793 1,611 Enclosure Acts were passed . . . the final steps in the process of enclosure came with the general Enclosure Acts of 1801, 1836 and 1845. Cambridge Historical Encyclopaedia of Great Britain and Ireland — Cambridge University Press 1985.

4. The CRE Appeal, brought against a publican for displaying a "No Travellers" sign, established that Gypsies are an ethnic minority within the meaning of the Race Relations Act. The judgement unfortunately made a distinction between Gypsies and other Travellers. However, the decision does extend to Travellers the protection of the legislation in relation to indirect discrimination, which is unlawful if it cannot be justified.

5. A manual system for registering information within the HPS. It consists of a white card which is "opened" on first contact and "closed" when the person referred to is housed or the Department's duty is discharged. It contains basic information on family membership, previous address, etc. It is intended as a viable progress record. However, because of organisation structures it proves virtually impossible to retain cards in a central holding place. Therefore information easily becomes inaccurate or incomplete. Cards get lost, mislaid or misplaced.

6. In fact, HPS opened to the public for a very short period and then reverted to a telephone service, mornings only. This has since been found to be

unlawful — Camden has not been fulfilling its responsibility under the Homeless Persons Act — see the *Guardian* 13.10.88.

7. So far as can be ascertained, Camden has only once withdrawn from a hotel — The Darlington Hotel, some time in 1987, for alleged racial harassment of a Bengali family.

8. All Council land is the responsibility of a particular Committee of the Council — for instance Leisure Committee is responsible for public open space; Housing Committee for housing estate land, etc.

9. A minority of Labour Councillors who resigned the Whip on the basis of non-agreement with the imposition of the cuts.

10. Section 1 of the Children and Young Persons Act 1963 provides for a discretionary power to enable financial assistance to be given to prevent the reception of children into care.

11. Attached to a memo dated 3.1.89 from the Assistant Valuer and Estates Surveyor correspondence was still being circulated concerning the proposed sale of this site.

12. Report to the Race and Community Relations Committee 24.10.84.

13. This is in fact a recommendation of the ALA report "Camden's Homelessness Policies and Procedures" April 1988.

Appendix I

London Borough of Camden Travellers: Current Policy

1. Members of the Travelling community have been visiting Camden for a considerable number of years. However, the Borough has no official sites, permanent or temporary, and the Council has in the past generally adopted the practice of evicting Travellers from its land as quickly as possible.

2. It is the view of the Commission for Racial Equality that Travellers are an ethnic group within the meaning of the Race Relations Act 1976. This view is shared by the Council's Race and Community Relations Committee which has, for the past 18 months, been actively developing a policy of non-harassment towards Travellers. The principal aims of the policy are to ensure that:
   a) Travellers are not discriminated against and are guaranteed equal access to services etc;
   b) the needs of Travellers are fully met;
   c) the rights of Travellers to their way of life is respected and understood by other Camden residents.

3. The key features of the Council's policy are:
   a) The Council will not seek to evict Travellers from its own land until such time as the land is required urgently for other uses;
   b) All Council departments are asked to endorse a non-harassment policy towards Travellers and to ensure that they are not acting in a discriminatory way towards Travellers;
   c) The provision of permanent and temporary sites in Camden;
   d) The Council will not use its 'designation' powers under the Caravan Sites Act 1968, except in exceptional circumstances.

4. The Council has established a Travellers Officers Group which meets regularly with Travellers' representatives to discuss how its policy can be effectively implemented and developed.

5. Guidelines have been drawn up which lay down the procedures to be followed when Travellers occupy land in Camden.
   a) *Council-owned Land:* If this is not urgently required for other uses,

80

arrangements will normally be made for temporary use as an 'unofficial' Travellers site and provision made for refuse collection, fresh water and toilet facilities. If the site is required urgently for other uses or is maintained for amenity use, eg public open space, the Council will seek repossession through the Courts, but only on the authority of a Chair's action and after a full report has been made by Council officers, including the Principal Race Relations Advisor. Basic facilities (refuse collection, water supply and toilets) will be provided where possible pending eviction.

b) *Housing Land:*

i) When Travellers arrive on a Council estate, and where the properties in the block/estate are for letting and any squatters would be immediately evicted, the Housing Department after consultation with the Central Race Relations Unit would apply for a possession order as soon as possible;

ii) If the block or estate is one from which squatters would not normally be evicted, then under normal circumstances relevant councillors would be informed of the situation and no action taken to repossess the site until a meeting had been held between the relevant councillors and officers. An eviction could only proceed with the agreement of the Committee Chairs.

c) *Other Land (eg privately owned):* The owner(s) will be advised of the Council's policy and encouraged to adopt similar procedures to those outlined in a) above. The Council will only use its 'designation' powers in exceptional circumstances.

6. A Travellers Outreach Worker is soon to be appointed in the Central Race Relations Unit to co-ordinate and develop the Council's policy on Travellers.

7. The Council is taking active steps to identify and develop a suitable permanent site for the use of Travellers arriving in Camden. There are already several permanent sites in Inner London and experience shows that when well-designed and efficiently run, they can be easily accommodated into densely developed urban areas such as Camden.

8. The Council believes that its non-harassment policy benefits not only the Travellers themselves, but minimises nuisance and ultimate cost to the ratepayer. If basic amenities were not provided on sites the result would be greater risks to the health and welfare of the Travellers, particularly for children, and additional cost to the Council in clearing up sites after any evictions. Similarly, the policy of allowing Travellers to remain on certain Council-owned sites enables better provision to be made for the welfare of Travellers in terms of access to education services. It also means that it is in the interests of the Travellers to maintain such sites in a good condition. If they are constantly evicted they have no such interest. They simply move to other unofficial sites leading to considerably greater nuisance and cost to the ratepayer.

6 February 1985

Appendix II

Queen's Bench Divisional Court

R v Bristol City Council ex parte Brown
21 June 1979

Mrs Browne arrived in this country from Eire with her seven children in March 1979. On doctor's advice she had left her home in Tralee because of her husband's violence and had gone to a Women's Aid Hostel in Limerick.

Some four months later her husband discovered her whereabouts. So the people in charge made arrangements for her to go to Bristol and stay in the Women's Aid Refuge there.

She spent the first night in the Refuge, but unfortunately the accommodation they had hoped to provide was taken up by emergency admissions. The next day Mrs Browne presented herself as homeless to the local authority.

The council arranged temporary accommodation in a guest house while they made their inquiries. An officer contacted the Community Welfare Officer in Tralee who said that accommodation would be provided if the family returned. That was confirmed in a second telephone conversation with another officer when the Community Welfare Officer also indicated that he was fully aware of the applicant's background.

A senior officer in Bristol concluded that they were obliged to secure accommodation for the family under Section 4(5). Although there was no local connection with Bristol they could not transfer responsibility under Section 5 because there was also no connection with any housing authority in England, Wales or Scotland. These findings were set out in their Section 8 notification.

From the conversation with Tralee he also concluded that the authorities there would not have agreed to the applicant returning if they were unable to protect her from any risk of violence. Consequently the council could meet their duty under Section 6(1)(c) by "giving . . . such advice and assistance as will secure that [s]he obtains accommodation from some other person".

In a report to the housing committee it was recommended that the applicant be advised to return to Tralee and contact the Community Welfare Officer there. The council would arrange for travel assistance. The committee agreed.

Mrs Browne was told of the decision and an appointment was made with the DHSS to provide her with a travel warrant. She made it clear that she did not want to return to Eire and did not go to the DHSS.

The housing committee then decided to stop payments to the guest house. So these were made by Bristol Women's aid and Shelter until legal proceedings started.

In April the High Court granted leave to apply for judicial review. Mrs Browne reapplied to the local authority. They gave her a Section 8 notification, identical to the first, and provided bed and breakfast accommodation for a few days, while insisting that they had already discharged their duty.

At the full hearing Lloyd J. said "it is clear beyond any doubt that the council has given such advice and offered such assistance (although it has not been accepted) as would enable the Applicant to obtain accommodation from . . . the Community Welfare Officer in Tralee".

In most cases the "person" in Section 6(1)(c) would be someone within the authority's area, but there was nothing in the Act to expressly confine it to that. Indeed the applicant had accepted that the council could fulfil their duty in this way, even though Tralee was outside the jurisdiction of the Act.

Instead the applicant had argued that Section 5(4)(b) ought to be applied by way of analogy, and she should not be returned to an area where she ran the risk of domestic violence.

Lloyd J. accepted the applicant had suffered violence in Tralee in the past. But that did not necessarily mean that she would suffer any risk of violence on her return. She would obviously not return to the same house, but there was other accommodation in the same area.

The risk involved was a matter for the council to consider, together with the Community Welfare Officer in Tralee. The authority had carefully considered it and there was no evidence on which the Court could interfere.

The Applicant had also contended that the accommodation offered was not sufficiently defined or specific, and so did not meet the requirements of Section 16. The judge rejected that submission. "The Council has satisfied itself that the accommodation will be available if the Applicant returns to Ireland. It was not incumbent on the Council to identify the particular house in question which the Community Welfare Officer in Ireland had in mind" [see R v Wyre Borough Council ex parte Parr].

Lord Widgery, the Lord Chief Justice, agreed and the application for mandamus was rejected.

(1979) 3 All ER 344; (1979) 1 WLR 1437 123 SJ 489; 130 NLJ 551; 143 LGR 508; 144 LGR 141; LAG September 1979 212; 1980 SCOLAG 151; 1980 JSWL 52.

Appendix III
Circular S50/85

Verification of Identity — Preventing Fraud

THE PROBLEM
1. There has been increasing concern about the payment of large amounts of Supp B, sometimes over a long period, to people using fictitious identities. This circular highlights and expands existing instructions on verification of identity.

ALL CLAIMS
2. On all claims it is necessary to establish on the balance of probabilities that the claimant is using his true identity. In most cases the claimant's identity can be satisfactorily established from the last wage slips or LO, NI, UBO or LA records. Under no circumstances should payment be made by default simply because of difficulty in obtaining evidence.

SUSPICIOUS CLAIMS
3. Take particular care to verify identity if the claimant —
   (1) has newly arrived in the area (including people from abroad);
   (2) lives in a hostel, hotel or a multi-occupied boarding/rooming house (there have been a number of recent fraud cases);
   (3) has no wage slips or means of verifying the last wages;
   (4) provides brand new documents such as copy of the birth certificate, Building Society passbook etc (these may have been acquired for a fraudulent claim).

HOW TO CONFIRM IDENTITY
Last Earnings
4. Verification of the last two wages usually establishes the claimant's identity. Verify the last two wages by —
   (1) examining wage slips, or
   (2) asking the claimant to get a statement from the employer, or
   (3) phoning the employer or sending them form A15.
Check if the wage slips are genuine and contact the employer if in doubt. If the claimant provides a phone number and the employer is unknown to you, consider the possibility that the phone number may be the claimant's (or a friends).

LO Records

5. (1) If a contributory NI benefit has been awarded or is in payment this is sufficient proof of identity.

(2) Where no NI benefit is in payment check LO, NI, UBO, or LA records to see if they can confirm the claimant's identity. If a claim for UB has not been rated, the UBO may not have established the claimant's identity even though an NI number is given on the BI or BIC. Check with the UBO to find out if the NI number has been verified with Newcastle Records. The existence of a National Insurance account can be checked by sending form MF64 to Newcastle Records (see Contributions Code 970-995 and CC57).

(4) If it is not possible to confirm the claimant's identity or there is still some doubt, ask the claimant to produce evidence of identity.

Documentary Evidence of Identity

6. The following documents can contribute to confirming a claimant's identity —

(1) Driving licence — a full licence is good evidence as it is difficult to obtain one improperly.

(2) LA rent book.

(3) Mortgage repayment documents.

(4) Fuel etc bills — addressed to the claimant at their home.

(5) Cheque guarantee card — also ask to see the associated personal cheque book.

(6) Sub-contractor's tax certificates — a form P714 has a photograph of the person to whom it was issued.

(7) Birth and Marriage certificates — do not accept a recently issued *copy* certificate on its own as no check is made on the person's identity. There have been many cases of claimants using forged birth certificates.

(8) Irish UB 15s and UA 22s — The UB15 is a buff coloured unemployment benefit card. The UA22 is a pink card issued to people claiming unemployment assistance (Irish Supp B).

(9) National Insurance Numbers — the lack of a NI number may be a reason for making further enquiries. Anyone who has been employed, or left school since 1975 should have a NI number. NI numbers can be confirmed from —

(a) Form P45 — the claimant should give the form to the UBO;

(b) P60 — the annual certificate of pay and tax deducted;

(c) NI card — some self-employed people still use stamps to pay contributions.

(10) Passports — only ask to see a passport if there is no other way of confirming identity. Do not insist on seeing the passport or give the impression that the request is a means of checking the claimant's right of residence in the UK.

See S3951 for the procedures for foreign nationals.

DO NOT ACCEPT THESE DOCUMENTS ON THEIR OWN

7. (1) A doctor's statement — doctors do not check a person's identity and medical certificates are sometimes stolen or forged.

(2) Non LA rent books — "Challenge" or "Albert" type rent books can be bought from newsagents and the entries could have been made by the claimant. Make a note of the landlord's name, address and phone number and contact the landlord in doubtful cases.
(3) Baptismal certificates — these are easily obtained or forged.
(4) NHS medical cards — the Family Practitioner Committee do not always check identity. Forged cards have been used.
(5) Travel passes — although many of these have photographs, it is unlikely that identity will have been checked.

NO EVIDENCE OF IDENTITY — INTERVIEWING THE CLAIMANT

8. Documentary evidence is genuinely unavailable only in a small number of cases. If a claimant does not provide adequate evidence or if you have reason to be suspicious, interview them in order to build up a picture of their recent history. If the interview fails to provide a means of confirming identity, the AO should consider whether the evidence is reliable taking into account the consistency and probability of the story. If evidence is not immediately available but can be acquired, consider a UNP.

9. Make enquiries along the following lines —
(1) Some claimants may state they have no wage slips because they have been doing casual work. Vagueness about last employment is often intended to hide the fact that the claim is fraudulent. A claimant who has recently finished work can reasonably be expected to remember the name of the last employer. If the claimant rarely works the last job should stick in their mind. Ask for the name, address and telephone number of the employer and write down the answers in the claimant's presence. Do this even if the last employment was outside the UK.
(2) If the claimant has not worked for some time there will probably have been previous claims for benefit, either in this country or abroad. If these have not been declared question the claimant about it. Check with the previous LO and send A51 appropriate. If there has been a previous claim, check the statement for consistency.
(3) If the claimant has a partner or children, it may be possible to check their identities from their NI numbers of CHB claims. This will contribute to a confirmation of the claimant's own identity.
(4) Has the claimant ever been in hospital? Does the claimant have any documents relating to medical treatment?
(5) Has the claimant been in touch with other bodies such as social services or the probation service?
(6) If the claimant states he has been receiving benefit in another country, ask for details and note them in the CP.

IF YOU SUSPECT A FALSE IDENTITY

10. If you believe that the claimant is using a false identity refer the CP to the fraud officer. Contact HQ (RD6B) by sending form A171 or by phone if the information is needed quickly. Refer to FIG 683-705.

PIU(E) for RD5B, December 1985   Distribution: Holders of S Manual